Golf

Golf

DETTY MOORE, M.S.
Instructor, Department of Health, Kinesiology, and Dance
Lamar University
Beaumont, Texas
LPGA, Class A

SERIES EDITOR
SCOTT O. ROBERTS, PH.D.
Department of Health, Physical Education, and Recreation
Texas Tech University
Lubbock, Texas

Boston, Massachusetts Burr Ridge, Illinois Dubuque, Iowa
Madison, Wisconsin New York, New York San Francisco, California St.Louis, Missouri

WCB/McGraw-Hill

A Division of The **McGraw·Hill** *Companies*

GOLF

Recycled paper

 This book is printed on recycled paper containing 10% postconsumer waste.

1 2 3 4 5 7 8 9 0 QPD QPD 9 0 9 8 7

Library of Congress Catalog Number: 97-70836

ISBN 0–8151–6859–4

Executive director: *Kevin Kane*
Publisher: *Ed Bartell*
Executive editor: *Vicki Malinee*
Developmental editor: *Alyssa Naumann*
Marketing manager: *Pamela S. Cooper*
Project manager: *Terry Routley*
Production supervisor: *Cheryl Horch*
Designer: *David Zielinski*
Cover design: *Barbara J. Hodgson*
Cover photograph: *Bill Leslie*
Series photographer: *James Crnkovich*
Illustrator: *Billy Moore*
Compositor: *Shepherd, Inc.*
Typeface: *10/12 Palatino*
Printer: *Quebecor*

http://www.mhcollege.com

DEDICATION

In Memory of My Parents

To my mother and best friend for her unconditional love and understanding. To my father for his enthusiasm for my golf and his continued support for my golfing endeavors. To both of them for their work and sacrifice to educate all of us and prepare us for a world in which I look forward to each day with excitement.

FOREWORD

Golf is a sport that you can work on learning for your entire life! And often, even enjoy that work! All of us who teach this game realize how important it is for everyone to get good sound fundamentals in the basic skills of the game.

How lucky you are to have a skilled and experienced professional teacher of the game share the information in this book with you. You may be assured of the fact that you're getting the very best information, presented in a way that you would receive it if you were getting a private lesson with a professional.

Detty Moore combines years of teaching physical skills with a well-developed talent of understanding the golf swing and the golf game. I first met Detty in 1984 when she came to work for me while I was Director of Education for the National Golf Foundation. Detty was completing a graduate degree in Sports Administration and needed "work experience" credits. She had determined that the NGF was the perfect place to combine her two loves . . . teaching and golf. And I quickly learned that she already knew a great deal about both these areas. Her contributions to the educational programs of the Foundation are still evident today.

Since that time, Detty has expanded her talents through numerous educational seminars, golf schools, clinics and independent study experiences. She has served as clinician and instructor in some of the most prestigious golf schools in America, among them the Gillette-LPGA Executive Women Golf Clinic Series and Peggy Kirk Bell's "Golfari" Golf Schools. She has participated in National Golf Foundation seminars for professionals, teachers, and coaches of the game. And she has taught an infinite number of group and individual golf lessons.

All the while she has never ceased learning golf herself. The results of her hard work in gaining ever higher levels of expertise as a teacher and player is found here in this book. She has used her knowledge to make the teaching and learning experience efficient and enjoyable for both instructor and student.

No one is better equipped to help you start or continue your journey toward playing better golf than this Irish lass, Detty Moore. Detty can give you information to use for a lifetime in this game of a lifetime.

Read, learn, and enjoy . . . golf and Detty Moore!

Annette Thompson
LPGA Master Professional
Past President,
LPGA Teaching and Club Professional Division

PREFACE

▶ Audience

This text is designed for anyone who enjoys playing golf and for students in academic courses in golf. This book is intended to be an easy-to-read, useful tool that provides information about how to develop and improve your game.

▶ Features

The intent of this book is to provide a basis for the beginner, intermediate, and advanced golfer alike to develop and improve the skills, which will ultimately make them better golfers. It contains sound fundamentals on everything from how to get started on the golf course to physical and mental goals. Chapter 1, What's Golf All About?, details a brief history of the sport and discusses its recent developments. Chapter 2 then begins to unfold the basic components of the game, such as the necessary equipment, rules, and your first trip to the golf course. In this text, you will learn about the basics of putting, chipping, pitching, ball flight, and how to overcome common problems. Specific skills and drills are included throughout the book to help you increase your level of play. This book has been adapted for the right- and left-handed golfer.

In addition, the text offers the following special features, which enhance its use:
- Each chapter has a bulleted list of objectives and a closing summary to reinforce the major points covered.
- Key terms are highlighted in boldface type and are defined in the text. This will enable you to build a working vocabulary of concepts and principles necessary for beginning, developing, and maintaining your game.
- Special Performance Tip boxes outline techniques, skills, and strategies for quick reference.
- Assessments appear at the end of applicable chapters to assist you in evaluating your skills and game performance.
- Appendices (A, B, and C) provide key golf terms, rules, and practice drills to help players understand and improve their game.
- Professional studio photographs illustrate proper techniques for effective play.

▶ Ancillaries

To facilitate the use of this text in the classroom, a printed Test Bank of approximately 100 questions is available to instructors. These multiple choice questions allow for quick assessment of the basic rules and principles of golf.

▶ **Acknowledgments**

I would like to thank the following reviewers, who provided me with expert commentary during the development of this text.

David Cameron, Ed.D.
Cameron University

Alan J. Stockholm, Ed.D.
SUNY, Cortland

Sandra Norton
University of Wisconsin, Madison

I would also like to extend a special thanks to all the students who crossed my path during the last twenty years. The students of St. Michael's, Finglas, Dublin, Ireland; Muckross Park, Dublin, Ireland; Lithgow High School, New South Wales, Australia; and Lamar University, Beaumont, Texas, have guided me and are responsible for the teacher that I am today.

My golf teaching career was influenced by two people in particular, Annette Thompson and Sandra Eriksson. Sandra's assistance in helping me stay and work in this country proved invaluable. Every aspect of my professional life is better because of Annette Thompson's influence and expert guidance. Special thanks to both of you.

No teacher evolves her own style without learning from various masters and mentors. In this learning, one takes the best of what they say and do and gives it her own flavor. For the history, many of the drills, exercises and concepts within this book, I thank those other teachers who have taught me. Among those are the contributors to the National Golf Foundation Educational Programs, United States Golf Association, the Ladies Professional Golf Association Educational program and the Sports Enhancement Associates Program. Specific individuals from whom many of the drills and information came include Linda Bunker, De De Owens, Conrad Rehling, Pat Lange, Pat Park, Gary Wiren, Lynn Marriott, David Witt, Peggy Kirk Bell, Carol Johnson and Ann Casey Johnstone.

I would like also to thank all the friends who helped me to produce this book. My brother Billy Moore; Graphics Place, Dublin, Ireland; Linda Hebert, Beaumont, Texas; Annette Thompson, Jupiter, Florida; Sandra Eriksson, Wellington, Florida; Lynn Castle, Curator of Exhibitions and Collections, Art Museum of Southeast Texas; Michelle Bell, LPGA Tour; Tracy Silverberg, Lamar University; Harold Blackwell, Lamar University; Theresa Flowers, Lamar University; Anne Huff, Beaumont, Texas; Hans Kohler, General Manager, Beaumont Country Club, David Burelson, PGA; Arthur Fontenot, Beaumont Country Club, and to all of you not mentioned who answered so many questions. Special thanks to Kim Brozer, Futures Tour, and Ron DeBlanc and Gerald Mathews, Lamar University, for demonstrating the specific techniques.

—Detty Moore

CONTENTS

1   What's Golf All About? 1
2   Your Personal Equipment: Vital to the Game, 6
3   How to Get Started: On the Course, 20
4   The Rules of Golf, 26
5   The Perfect Swing: Skills, 42
6   Basics of Putting: Technique, 57
7   Basics of Chipping: Technique, 75
8   Basics of Pitching: Technique, 87
9   The Full Swing: Skills, 96
10 Understanding Ball Flight: Common Problems, 117
11 Hitting Sand Shots: Skills, 125
12 Understanding Uneven Lies: Strategy, 134
13 Conditioning: Physical and Mental, 145
14 Setting Goals: Physical and Mental, 153
15 Managing Your Game on the Course, 157

Appendix A Golf Terms, 167
Appendix B Rules Simplified, 173
Appendix C Thirty-Ball Routine, 181
Suggested Readings, 183

Golf

CHAPTER 1

WHAT'S GOLF ALL ABOUT?

OBJECTIVES

After reading this chapter, you should be able to do the following:

- Discuss the history of golf.
- Outline the contributions golf makes toward lifetime wellness.

KEY TERMS

While reading this chapter, you will become familiar with the following terms:

- ► Commons
- ► Forecaddies
- ► Gorse
- ► Heather
- ► Heaths
- ► Links
- ► Parkland

INTRODUCTION TO GOLF

A COMMON GOLF DAYDREAM

It's the final day of a major golf tournament, and you come to the par four eighteenth hole tied for the lead. You pull out a wedge for your approach shot and land it two feet left of the hole. The crowd goes wild and roars their appreciation as you walk up to the green. Calming your nerves you line up your putt, relax, and swing back and through straight into the hole.

All of us have this dream, although we do not get to realize it like Jack Nicklaus, Tom Watson, Seve Ballesteros, Laura Davies, Beth Daniel, and many others. What we do have in common with the golfing greats is a desire to learn how to play and how to improve.

HISTORY OF GOLF

The origin of golf is unknown, but there are a number of theories. Golf historian Peter Dobereiner dates the first match as far back as 1296 in the village of Loenen in Holland. Golf was reported in France, Belgium, and Holland in Roman times. The Scots are responsible for spreading the game throughout the world. They may not have invented the game of golf, but they certainly can take credit for its development. Golf was becoming such an obsession in Scotland that in 1457 King James II banned golf, claiming that archery should be practiced for the defense of the country and golf was distracting from it.

Golf, as we know it, can be dated back to Scotland in 1744. The basic rules were drafted in 1754 at the Royal and Ancient Golf Club of St. Andrews. The introduction of golf in the United States was in Yonkers, New York, in 1888, and the United States Golf Association was established in 1894. The United States Golf Association, in conjunction with the Royal and Ancient Golf Club of St. Andrews, is the official governing body that dictates and interprets the rules of play.

DEVELOPMENTS

Equipment and golf courses continue to improve because of technology. Mary Queen of Scots, the game's most famous female player during her time, was outnumbered by the men playing the sport. Today the game is played worldwide by men, women, and children, both amateurs and professionals. Professionals participate on the PGA, LPGA, Senior Tours, and numerous minitours. To gain a card to play on any of these tours, players must go through many grueling rounds of qualifying. Those who succeed at Qualifying School are outnumbered by those who do not succeed. Most of these unsuccessful players because of the nature of the game, will work on their game to gain a card for the big tour the next year. In the meantime, they will play on one of the numerous minitours or on the European, Australian, or Asian tours.

Golf is society's fastest growing leisure activity. The game is played on manicured courses, a major improvement from the cow, sheep, and goat fields of the Scottish highlands. Here young shepherds passed the long hours hitting a piece of wood through the natural landscape thick with **heather, gorse,** and sand dunes. The scenery was beautiful, but the manicured courses today are an improvement. The terrain over which golf is now played are **links** and **parkland.** There is an Irish proverb, "To know beauty one must live with it." Surely there is no better way to savor the country's beautiful landscapes than to rise with the birds and play golf with the hares. Many courses provide an unforgettable experience through great golf and visual splendor. The word "breathtaking" would seem a mild description if you could stand in the wind at Pebble Beach, California, United States; Ballybunion, Ireland; or St. Andrews, Scotland, and savor their uniqueness. Golf offers an opportunity to relax and socialize in an atmosphere of peace, serenity, and tranquility.

TRENDS

Courses, equipment, and clothing have changed over the years. Courses of the twentieth century differ from the open **heaths** and **commons** of Scotland. Early Scottish courses had no boundaries and **forecaddies** went ahead to clear the way for the golfers. Players would play out to a predesignated target and back in to another target. Thus the terms "out" for the first nine and "in" for the back or second nine holes in an 18-hole round of golf were derived. It was difficult to differentiate between fairway and green!

► **Heather**
A plant with green leaves and purple-pink flowers common to the Scottish highlands where the game of golf began.

► **Gorse**
A prickly shrub with a yellow flower, also common to the Scottish highlands.

► **Links**
Golf courses by the seashore that incorporate natural dunes and grasses.

► **Parkland**
A kind of golf course terrain that is inland and wooded and may include lakes or streams.

► **Heaths**
A tract of open wasteland covered with shrubs and heather; the game of golf was first played on the heaths and commons of Scotland.

► **Commons**
An area of land shared by many people.

► **Forecaddies**
The name given to people who carried golf clubs for golfers.

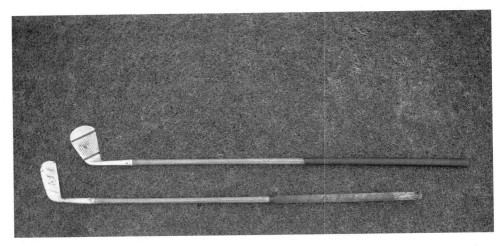

FIGURE 1-1 Hickory shaft clubs like these have been replaced by shafts of steel, graphite, boron, and titanium.

The equipment used in the twentieth century is as diverse as the people playing the game. The days of the *feathery* ball and the *hickory* shaft (see figure 1-1) have long disappeared. The original ball was made of wood; by the seventeenth century the feathery ball became popular. This ball, as the name implies, was constructed from feathers that were wet down and covered with cowhide, stitched and pulled tight. The feathery ball was replaced by the *gutta-percha* ball in the nineteenth century. This ball was made of rubber and it carried longer distances, but not necessarily straight. The flat surface had to be replaced with a dimpled surface for more predictable ball flight. Research continues to find the best pattern of dimples for greatest ball flight. The feathery and gutta-percha balls have been replaced with balls to suit the individual's game. The young shepherd boy would have used a stick to propel an object across the dunes. The stick has evolved over the centuries, from blackthorn wood to hickory wood, which gives the shaft its name. These hickory shafts were used well into the twentieth century. Original shafts have been replaced by shafts of steel, graphite, boron, and titanium. The clothing has also changed over the years. Women were at a greater disadvantage than men when it came to clothing, because they had to deal with bonnets, flouncy blouses, long full skirts, and corsets! Surely their golf attire was a severe handicap.

GOLF AS A LIFETIME SPORT

Golf is a lifetime sport played for pleasure and business by millions of men, women, and children worldwide. Golf can be played from a very young age and continue well into old age. Golf is fun, relaxing, challenging, and extremely social. The challenge can be exciting and humiliating. The game can be played competitively and socially. Golf is possibly the only game where the beauty and layout of the playing area changes with each shot. Unfortunately, some golfers forget to take time to "smell the roses." Many people also use golf for stress release. It may be their only form of exercise. When young people take up golf, the game helps build character. What other game is the player the sole rules official as in golf? Young people learn about honesty and integrity, which show character on and off the golf course. Finally, the game is both a mental and physical challenge. Young and old learn to perform well mentally under pressure, which carries over in all aspects of life.

GOLF ON VACATION

A good way to explore a country and its history is through golf and the eyes of the locals. Try planning a golf vacation in a foreign country; travel in the off season, when golf is less expensive; and learn about the area's unique history. This is a great way to see and appreciate the country. It is relatively easy to combine a golf and historical trip to the rugged courses of Scotland, Ireland, and England. While there be sure to inhale the country's beauty, splendor, and history.

SUMMARY

- The game of golf dates back to the thirteenth century.
- The Scots are responsible for developing and perpetuating the game of golf as we know it.
- Equipment and golf courses continue to improve because of technology.
- Golf is society's fastest growing leisure activity.
- Golf is a sport that can be practiced and enjoyed over a lifetime.

CHAPTER 2

YOUR PERSONAL EQUIPMENT:
VITAL TO THE GAME

OBJECTIVES

After reading this chapter, you should be able to do the following:

- Outline the kinds of equipment a beginner needs.
- Determine the financial outlay necessary to begin golfing.
- Recognize that different clubs suit different ability levels.
- Discuss the proper care of golfing equipment.

KEY TERMS

While reading this chapter, you will become familiar with the following terms:

- ► Irons
- ► Woods

Performance Tip

Overall Equipment/Outfitting Needs

All golfers should have:

1. A rules book
2. A bag
3. Clubs
4. Golf shoes
5. Golf balls
6. Tees
7. A plug mark repairer tool
8. Appropriate clothing: look smart and comfortable

FACILITIES AND EQUIPMENT

Jeans, very short shorts, and tank tops are inappropriate and not allowed on the majority of golf courses because golf courses have and enforce a strict dress code. The items mentioned in this chapter are necessities. Other items may be added, such as a golf glove. The glove may enhance the grip, especially in hot weather when hands perspire. Right-handed golfers wear the glove on the left hand. Left-handed golfers wear the glove on the right hand. A waterproof suit is a must for winter golf. A golf umbrella could come in handy, provided conditions are not too gusty or there is not a forecast for lightning. A pull cart is a great investment for the golfer who prefers to walk rather than ride.

PERSONAL EQUIPMENT

CLUBS

There are so many clubs and price ranges on the market that purchasing equipment can be confusing. It is best for the beginning golfer to consult a local professional who will recommend clubs suitable to the individual's ability and price range. Equipment for the beginner may differ in set make up from that of the intermediate or advanced student. The beginner will not require all fourteen clubs that comprise a full set. A partial set will be sufficient to get the beginner out to the golf course.

It is important for the beginner to become familiar with all the available clubs and their uses. The rules of golf allow a player to carry fourteen clubs. These would be a combination of **woods, irons** and a putter. When purchasing a set of clubs, it is best to buy those that look and feel good, while keeping the following components in mind: grip, shaft flex, length, club head lie, and swing weight. This means it is important to hit clubs, preferably on a range, before buying them.

▶ Grip

There is a variety of grips to choose from and the same grip will not suit every golfer. The material used in the grip, whether leather, rubber, synthetic, half cord, or full cord, should suit the individual's preference. Grips (see figure 2-5) are important because hands placed correctly on the grip are the only contact the golfer has with the club. The game of golf is difficult enough without using grips that are worn or ill fitting. The way a player holds the club equals a square face, which equals square contact with the ball. All this prepares the player for square contact. Feel is most important and a "tacky" grip is helpful to achieving proper feel. Feel is the sense that the club is an extension of the hands and that one is able to effortlessly execute all shots, especially the shots from just off the green. Most players have a preference in texture and feel of the grip. Of equal importance is correct grip size. Too small or too large a grip creates tension and affects the release of the hands, which in turn will influence ball flight. Check the grip size by gripping the club with the normal grip and then remove the rear (nontarget) hand. The middle fingers of the target hand (left hand for right-handed golfers) should just touch the palm (reverse for the left-handed golfer). If the fingers dig into the palm, the grip is too small. If there is a gap between the fingers and the palm, the grip is too big.

▶ Shaft Flex

The two most common shaft materials used are steel and graphite. The primary concern should be the flex of the shaft. The purpose of the shaft is not only to connect the head of the club and the grip but, more importantly, to flex and reflex to the rhythm style of the player's swing. This allows a player to experience the ease of that perfect powerful shot using the least amount of effort. The range in shafts is from flexible to very stiff; the most flexible is *L*, or ladies', and the stiffest is *XX stiff*. Flex should be suited to the golfer's ability and the speed and style of the swing. The standard ladies set has " L" or "A" semiflexible shafts. The standard

▶ Woods

Golf clubs with wooden heads used to hit the ball long distances. Wooden heads have been replaced with metal heads.

▶ Irons

Golf clubs with metal heads, numbered from 1 to SW according to their degree of slant, used to hit the ball with precision.

men's set has an "R" or regular shaft. The very strong golfer with a fast swing would use an "S" or stiff shaft. As the player gets older and slows down, the more flexible shaft will be a better choice. Most players are in the L, A, or R range. Never assume what you need until you try a range of clubs and make comparisons.

▶ Length

The proper length of the club is determined by a number of factors including the golfer's height, length of arms, posture, playing style, and ability. Having the proper length of club has a direct bearing on making solid contact with the ball and the center of the club face. Seek the advice of a professional when buying clubs; it will only take the pro a short time to fit clubs. This is worth the time and effort. The professional will get you to swing clubs of various lengths, flex, lies, and grips to determine the club best suited to your physique and swing.

▶ Club Head Lie

Proper club head lie is a critical issue and a must for good play (see figure 2-1). It is dictated by posture to the ball, length of arms, and height. A player's lie, as with other club-fitting factors, varies from player to player. The lie of a club can only be checked dynamically—having a player hit balls off a lie board to see if an

FIGURE 2-1 Proper club head lie is a must for good play.

adjustment is necessary. The angle between the shaft and the head of the club can be adjusted for a player's lie. A lie too flat or too upright will affect ball flight. All professionals can quickly check and have clubs adjusted for each golfer.

▶ Swing Weight

Swing weight is the relationship between the length, head weight, and grip weight. Swing weight is used to check that all clubs in the set will feel the same when the player swings.

Overall weight is a more important consideration when selecting clubs. Choose a club that does not feel too heavy or too light. If the club is too heavy, the golfer will be unable to create enough club head speed to gain distance. Heavy clubs will also cause rapid fatigue. On the other hand, if the clubs are too light, the player will be unable to get enough "punch" in the shot and will also sacrifice distance. Choose a club that you feel you can swing within yourself.

▶ Woods

The woods are numbered 1 (driver) through 5 (also, 6 wood through 9 wood can be special ordered). The club was originally made of a wooden head, thus the name (see figure 2-2). Persimmon or laminated heads were originally used rather than the now popular metal "woods." The number 1 wood, or driver, has a long shaft and less loft on the face than any of the other woods. As the numbers increase, the loft on the club face increases and the length of the shaft decreases. The driver is designed to hit the ball the farthest distance, resulting in a long shot with a low trajectory. As you go through the 2, 3, 4, and 5 woods the shafts get shorter by ½ inch for each club and the club face becomes more lofted. The woods are designed to hit the ball a long distance. The 5 wood, the shortest of these wood clubs, still hits the ball a long way, with a higher trajectory because of the loft on the club face. Beginners should purchase a driver with a greater degree of loft on the club face; an example of this is a driver with face loft of 12 degrees rather than standard 11 degrees.

FIGURE 2-2 The club was originally made of a wooden head, thus the name, rather than the now popular metal "woods."

Performance Tip

A Good Start is a Strong Foundation for Future Success

Seeking professional advice in purchasing clubs is advisable. It is best for the beginner not to spend a fortune on clubs but rather use the money for professional instruction and advice. Initial progress and success depend on effective technique rather than equipment.

▶ Irons

The irons are numbered 1 through 9, pitching wedge (PW), and sand wedge (SW). Iron clubs are forged and cast. The earlier clubs were forged or blades. Each club head is heated and hammered into shape. There may be a slight difference between each head because of this process. These days most clubs are cast. The hot metal is poured into a mold and each club head is formed. These clubs are perimeter weighted with hollowed-out backs, which allows more weight on the sole and toe of the club (see figure 2-3). With the weight in the sole of the club, it helps the golfer get the ball in the air and hit a straighter shot when hit in the center or "sweet spot" of the face. The irons, like the woods, decrease in shaft length as the number increases. Most golfers do not use the 1 and 2 irons; these are only used by excellent male and female golfers. The 3 iron has a longer shaft and less face loft than the 4 iron, 5 iron through the SW. Similar to the woods, the irons decrease in length by ½ inch between clubs; as you get closer to the green (putting area) the club shaft will be shorter and the club face will have more loft. In the average set the 3 iron is the longest of the irons and propels the ball the farthest; the ball has

FIGURE 2-3 Today most iron clubs are cast and perimeter weighted with hollowed-out backs that allow more weight on the sole and toe of the club.

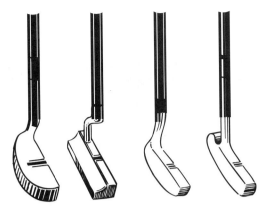

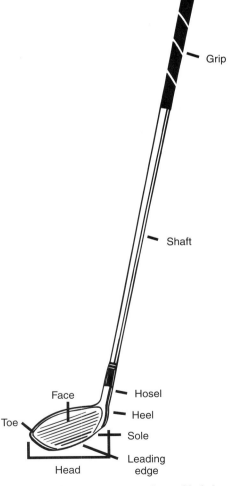

FIGURE 2-4 Putters do not come with the regular set of clubs and must be purchased separately. Consulting a professional will ensure that you select a putter with the correct length and lie, and one that is appropriate with your stance.

a low, long trajectory. The SW has a short, high trajectory. Intermediate and advanced golfers also carry a variety of wedges; these wedges have greater loft than the SW and are mostly used in the area surrounding the green.

▶ Putters

Putters come in many variations (see figure 2-4). When choosing a putter, keep in mind how you wish to stand to the ball. Your stance may dictate the type of putter. Putters have varied lengths and lies, therefore, you should seek the advice of the professional. The putter must suit your posture. The feel of the putter in your hands and the feel of the ball at impact is important. The putter does not come with the regular set; it must be purchased separately.

▶ Parts of a Golf Club

Figure 2-5 illustrates the parts of a golf club.

FIGURE 2-5 The parts of a golf club.

Performance Tip

Choosing Clubs as a Beginner

A beginner will certainly not need all fourteen clubs.
Many combinations are used, but a good set for beginners would be

- Woods 1, 3, 5 or 3, 5, 7
- Irons 3, 5, 7, 9, SW, and putter or 4, 6, 8, PW, SW, and putter.

The more intermediate-level golfer often carries

- Woods 1, 3, 4, 5
- Irons 3 through SW and putter
- Total 14 clubs.

▶ How Far Should I Be Able to Hit With Each Club?

Accuracy is more important than distance for all players. How far you hit the ball with each club is dependent on your ability. The approximate distance between each iron is about 10 yards (see figure 2-6). The 3 iron should travel 60 yards farther than the 9 iron. The woods again vary in distance and trajectory. The

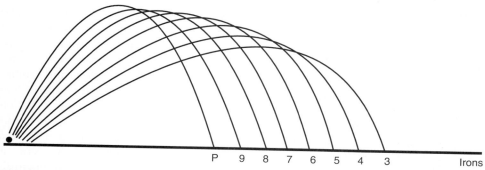

FIGURE 2-6 How far you hit the ball depends on your ability. The approximate distance between each iron is about 10 yards.

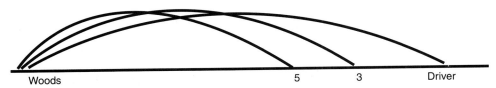

Woods   5   3   Driver

FIGURE 2-7 The distance between each wood is approximately 10 to 15 yards.

distance between each wood is approximately 10 to 15 yards (see figure 2-7). The beginner may find that the distance between clubs is much less than the estimated 10 yards, but with practice and good technique a swing with more consistent results will be achieved.

BALLS

There are balls to suit each individual's game. Balls are available for high trajectory, low trajectory, and distance. The ball may be *wound* or *solid* construction. The wound ball has a core of wound rubber, covered with either a balata, a sap from the bully tree, or a surlyn synthetic cover. The most durable ball has a surlyn cover and is the best type of ball for a beginner. It is difficult to mark or cut the surlyn cover. The ball may be marked or cut if it is hit above the center or equator. Balata balls, the usual choice of professionals, have softer and less durable covers. The solid ball is made with a solid synthetic core and a surlyn cover. This ball will be very durable, but because of its hardness will lose distance and the feel at contact will not be as crisp.

Compression is another important factor to consider when purchasing a golf ball. There is 100, 90, and 80 compression. When you play a 100 compression ball (distinguished by a black number on the ball), you may get more distance. However, you sacrifice the feel around the greens. By this I mean the contact of the ball on the club face. With 90 and 80 compression, you may not get the same distance but expect spin, which means the ball will stop faster and will feel softer off the club face. The 90 compression ball will feel softer than the harder 100 compression ball. Usually the stronger player will play the ball with the higher compression. The golfer should play the ball that feels best. This will be determined by a solid feeling at contact. For the beginning to average golfer, the type of ball or compression is irrelevant. Price will most likely dictate choice. The number on the ball is for identification purposes; if two players were playing the same brand ball, they would each play one with a different number, which eliminates the chance of hitting the wrong ball during play and incurring a two-stroke penalty. The color of the number on the ball identifies the compression. Red numbers indicate 90 or 80 compression, whereas black numbers indicate a 100 compression.

FIGURE 2-8 Tees are made of plastic or wood and vary in length.

TEES

You may tee up the ball on the teeing ground at the beginning of each hole. The ball is placed on a tee made of wood or plastic, and tees vary in length (see figure 2-8). To hit a ball with an iron, a shorter tee would be used.

GOLF BAGS

Bags come in numerous styles, sizes, and colors with a price range to suit everyone's needs (see figure 2-9). Your choice of bag will depend on whether you walk or drive a cart. The walker must also decide if he or she will carry the bag or use a pull cart. Larger bags are available for use on golf carts. These bags have an abundance of pockets for balls and clothing. Small carry bags may be used by walkers. These may be bags as slender as a pencil with pockets for balls and tees only or slightly larger with extra pockets for sweaters and waterproofs. These carry bags also come with a stand attached, helpful if the ground is wet; using the stand also provides easy access to the clubs. A wide padded strap is necessary for carrying the bag. A bag that is divided into sections is useful to keep short irons, long irons, putter, and woods divided. These dividers may be padded to save wear and tear on the shafts.

FIGURE 2-9 Your choice of golf bags will depend on whether you walk the course or drive a cart.

CARTS

Many walkers use pull carts; there are many varieties to choose from (see figure 2-10). The cart should be light, well balanced, and easy to dismantle for transportation. Most golf shops will rent a pull cart for a nominal fee. There are also battery-operated carts available, which require only a guiding hand. These are used by all ages, but especially seniors and those individuals with health problems. Many golfers prefer to ride a golf cart, either battery or gas operated (see figure 2-11).

CLOTHING

Golf is a gentlemen's and ladies' game, and men and women should dress appropriately. To add a psychological advantage, if you feel good about your appearance, you will feel better about yourself and your golf game. Attire should be neat and tidy, and if you are not certain about dress code (most clubs have one) just inquire. Women usually wear knee-length shorts, slacks, or skirt and blouse, with or without a collar. Men wear shirts with a collar and slacks or dress shorts. Tank tops, jeans, and cutoffs are not appropriate golfing attire as indicated by dress code provisions at each course. Bright colors are acceptable on the course. Wear clothes that look and feel good. It is also important to follow the clubhouse dress code.

FIGURE 2-10 A pull cart should be light, well balanced, and easy to dismantle for transportation.

FIGURE 2-11 Riding in a battery or gas operated cart allows seniors and individuals with health problems to enjoy golf when they otherwise might not be able to.

FOOTWEAR

Golf shoes come with or without spikes (cleats), in rubber, leather, and synthetic composition. Prices range from $20 to $1,000. The most important factor is comfort. A water-resistant leather shoe is ideal. I recommend shoes with spikes for firmer foot control, especially when ground conditions are wet (see figure 2-12). Certain courses recommend the popular soft-spikes, which are gentle on the green. Metal spikes may be replaced with soft-spikes in minutes at minimal cost. Thick, comfortable socks should be worn when purchasing new golf shoes because this type of sock will be worn when playing.

FIGURE 2-12 Golf shoes with spikes provide firm foot control.

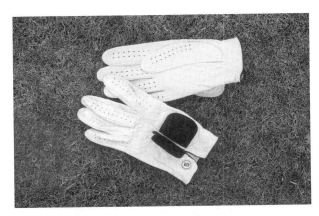

FIGURE 2-13 A glove may enhance grip, especially in hot weather when hands perspire.

WATERPROOFS

A waterproof suit should fit comfortably over clothes. The suit is necessary in wet weather and is desirable in cold conditions. Many golfers find wet gear restricting. Waterproofs need to be carried winter and summer, depending on where one plays; Ireland, for example, has unpredictable weather conditions. A wonderful tip for those golfers who find jackets restricting is to wear the waterproof trousers. If your back is warm, your flexibility will not be inhibited.

Wear layers on the top, maybe a T-shirt and turtleneck, over which you put a plastic dry cleaners bag (cut a hole for the neck and arms). On top wear a shirt and sweater. This keeps you toasty warm and dry (except for the outer layer), with freedom to swing.

GLOVE

A golfer may wear a glove (see figure 2-13). The glove may be leather, cloth, or a synthetic material. Some golfers remove the glove for putting, which may provide better feel.

CARE OF EQUIPMENT

Golf clubs or clothes should not be left in car trunks in very hot or cold weather. Heat, humidity, and cold will naturally affect the life of the equipment. Clubs should be cleaned after play. Use soapy water, wash and rinse the heads, and then dry with a towel. If grooves (lines) on the club face are dirty, use a tee or a similar object to remove dirt. Grips should be cleaned regularly to extend their life. Scrub with soapy water and a brush. When grips become shiny and lose their tacky feel, new grips are necessary. After golfing in the rain it is best to dry out all equipment. Clubs should be taken out of the bag and dried separately. Gloves, bag, waterproofs, shoes, and umbrella should also be dried. This procedure will prolong the life of your equipment and the equipment will also smell much better.

SUMMARY

- Among the important items needed by even beginning golfers are a rule book, a bag, clubs, golf shoes, golf balls, tees, a plug mark repair tool, and appropriate clothing.
- It is best for the beginning golfer to consult a local professional when choosing clubs.
- The rules of golf allow a player to carry up to 14 clubs—a combination of woods, irons, and a putter.
- It is best to keep the following components in mind when purchasing golf clubs: grip, shaft flex, length, club head lie, and swing weight.
- Parts of the golf club include the grip, shaft, head, heel, toe, face, sole, hosel, and the leading edge.
- Golf is a gentlemen's and ladies' game, and clothing should be neat, tidy, and appropriate.
- Taking good care of your golfing equipment will help prolong its life and usefulness.

CHAPTER 3

HOW TO **GET STARTED:**
ON THE COURSE

OBJECTIVES

After reading this chapter, you should be able to do the following:

- Understand that patience is a requirement for success at golf.
- Outline the basics for a solid foundation of golfing skills.
- Recognize where you can acquire professional help and guidance.
- Describe the various types of practice facilities.
- Demonstrate what to do before a round of golf.

KEY TERMS

While reading this chapter, you will become familiar with the following terms:

- ► Bunker
- ► Chipping
- ► Executive Courses
- ► LPGA
- ► Par
- ► PGA
- ► Putting

GETTING STARTED

Getting started in the game of golf is a very exciting time. Whatever age you are when you take up the sport, be realistic about your goals. For many reasons, whether it be social or financial, the majority of golfers do not take up the sport until later in life and cannot comprehend why their performance level is not quite like that of a professional. Some professionals were swinging cut-down clubs as young as 3 years of age.

BE REALISTIC

Golf is a fun game but difficult and challenging. Approach the game with a positive, fun-loving attitude. Many successful athletes are not necessarily an overnight success at golf. Success comes from practice, knowledge of the skills, time, and patience.

LEARNING THE BASICS

Seek professional help for a solid foundation. You should take individual or group lessons. Your professional can team you up with people of equal playing ability. You may begin by joining a club, a business league, or a golf class at a university or on the driving range. Wherever you start, familiarize yourself with all aspects of the game. If you are unsure or nervous about starting, consult your **LPGA** (Ladies Professional Golf Association) or **PGA** (Professional Golfer Association) professional. These professionals are men and women who teach golf at public and private facilities all over the world. Call a local golf club or driving range for an appointment. They will put you on the right track.

DRIVING RANGES

Driving ranges are excellent facilities. Practice your skills on the driving range and then bring them to the course. To illustrate this point, a golf coach, after asking one of her regular players about a player new to the team, received the

► **LPGA**
The Ladies Professional Golf Association, which has both playing and teaching divisions.

► **PGA**
The Professional Golf Association of America, which is primarily made up of men, although women are accepted.

A

FIGURE 3-1 Driving range practice allows you to focus on all aspects of your game. **A,** main range, **B,** chipping, **C,** putting.

response, "Coach, she plays **par** golf on the range, but her game doesn't travel." Most ranges have long and short game facilities that include areas where you can hit woods and long irons and practice **chipping, bunker** play, and **putting** (see figure 3-1). Use all the clubs while on the driving range and practice with a purpose. If there is an option to hit from the grass rather than the Astroturf, do so. During winter or inclement weather watch golf on television or golf videos and practice your putting indoors. Many people are visual learners, and their golf

▶ **Par**
The standard of scoring for each hole, such as "a par 3 hole" or "a par 72 course." To play at par means that one is able to complete a hole or a course using no more strokes than par for that hole or course.

▶ **Chipping**
Making strokes just off the green that have more roll than air time.

▶ **Bunker**
A hazard covered with sand. Grass bordering the bunker or within the bunker is not considered part of the bunker. Often called a "trap" or a "sand trap."

▶ **Putting**
A pendulum swing on the putting green to place the ball into the hole.

B

C

game may improve by observing professionals. After the courtesies, rules, and etiquette have been learned and skills practiced, it is now time to go to the course. However, be certain to return to your teacher for a 3-, 6-, and 12-month physical!

YOUR FIRST TRIP TO THE GOLF COURSE

After you have sought the assistance of your professional on equipment and have outfitted yourself accordingly, it is time to make an exciting trip to the golf course. Caddy for an experienced golfer a few times before taking the plunge yourself; it would also be of tremendous benefit to play with an experienced player for one or two rounds of golf before you go out alone. If you are familiar with the rules of etiquette and you play with a friend who is experienced, you will be more relaxed and can put what you have learned into action. There are certain rules to keep in mind when you go to a public or private golf course for the first time. Public and private courses consist of 9-hole, 18-hole, par three's, and **Executive courses.** Many courses have a driving range facility you may use before the round. If there is no driving range, it is advisable to stretch and swing a club.

Performance Tip

Making the Most of Your First Trip to the Golf Course

Before your trip:

- Call ahead and reserve a tee time for the following day; it may be necessary to call a week in advance.

That day:

- Give yourself adequate time to pay the green fee.
- Rent a pull cart.
- Warm up and hit a bucket of balls.
- Practice putting.

▶ **Executive courses**
A golf course that is slightly shorter than a regulation course. There are some par four but mostly par three holes.

When on the course be aware of players behind you; beginners can speed up play by moving smartly between shots and between the green and tee box of the next hole. If a beginner is familiar with courtesy, rules, and etiquette, they have a right to be on the golf course just like any other golfer.

Private facilities are not quite as accessible as public courses. To play at a private course, you must be an invited guest of a member. Whether you play at a public or private facility, ask about a dress code for both on and off the course. This could save much embarrassment.

To become a member of a private club can be very expensive. There are many excellent public facilities, making private golf club membership unnecessary. Many public courses have ladies' and men's groups; by joining these groups you will meet playing partners quickly and make friends. Business leagues are also an option, so check at the pro shop. Whatever direction you choose to begin your endeavor, you will certainly find golf enjoyable.

SUMMARY

- Golf is an enjoyable game, but it can be difficult and challenging. Success in golf comes from practice, knowledge of the skills involved, time, and patience.
- Individual or group lessons can help establish a solid foundation of golfing skills.
- Driving ranges are good places to practice basic golfing skills before trying them out on a course.
- Membership in a private golf club is unnecessary; there are plenty of excellent public golf clubs.

CHAPTER 4

THE **RULES** OF GOLF

OBJECTIVES

After reading this chapter, you should be able to do the following:

- Recognize all areas from the tee to the green.
- Define the term "par."
- Understand that a knowledge of the rules of golf is to your advantage.
- Outline the primary types of competition in golf.
- Discuss how a golfer can establish a handicap.
- Identify the most common rules, infringements, and penalties in the game of golf.
- Describe the rules of etiquette and play.
- Follow safety procedures on the golf course and driving range.

KEY TERMS

While reading this chapter, you will become familiar with the following terms:

- ► Apron
- ► Bunkers (sand traps)
- ► Green
- ► Handicap
- ► Hazards
- ► Hole

- ► Honor
- ► Out of Bounds
- ► Tee
- ► Teeing Area
- ► Water Hazards

BASIC RULES AND ETIQUETTE OF PLAY

The game of golf is played on a course of 9 or 18 holes. The primary intent is to get the ball into the hole in as few shots as possible. Every hole will vary in length, but all holes consist of (1) teeing ground, (2) fairway, (3) rough, (4) hazards, and (5) putting green (see figure 4-1). Players hit their own balls from the **teeing area** and try to get the ball into the **hole** on the **green.**

The teeing area is identified by markers (see figure 4-2), and the ball is placed on a **tee** between the markers. This area usually has three sets of markers from which to play. Colored markers are used to distinguish "forward," "regular," and "championship" tees. Usually the forward tees are marked in red. The regular tees are marked in white. The back or championship tees are marked in blue.

The *fairway* is the closely mowed area between the tee and the green where all players attempt to land the ball. The *rough* is the longer grass on both sides of the fairway. The rough is best avoided because the grass is longer and thicker and it may be more difficult to place the ball on the green or fairway from there.

Bunkers (sand traps) and **water hazards** are known as **hazards** and are placed in strategic positions on each hole. Water hazards are classified as *lateral* or *regular*. Lateral water hazards run parallel to the fairway, and regular water hazards traverse the fairway.

▶ **Teeing Area**

The starting area for the hole being played. Also referred to as the "tee box." The teeing area is a rectangular patch of ground, bordered in the front by two markers and extending two club lengths in depth. The ball must be placed between the markers or back within two club lengths. The player may stand outside the teeing ground, but the ball must be inside.

▶ **Hole**

The 4.25 inch hole in the ground on the putting green, into which a golfer tries to get the ball in as few strokes as possible. Typical golf courses consist of either 9 or 18 holes.

▶ **Green**

The putting area of a given hole on the golf course.

▶ **Tee**

A small peg with a shallow top that holds a golf ball for an initial stroke.

▶ **Bunkers (sand traps)**

A hazard covered with sand. Grass bordering or within the bunker is not considered part of the bunker. Often called a "trap" or "sand trap."

▶ **Water Hazards**

Any sea, lake, pond, river, canal, ditch, or other open water within the confines of or adjacent to a golf course. Water hazards are marked with yellow stakes or yellow lines. Lateral hazards are marked with red stakes or red lines.

▶ **Hazards**

The term used for bunkers and water hazards on the course.

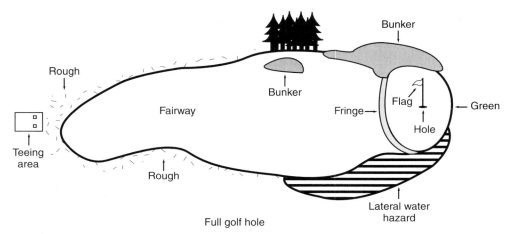

FIGURE 4-1 Each hole consists of a teeing ground, fairway, rough, hazards, and putting green.

FIGURE 4-2 The teeing area is always identified by markers. Some teeing areas have "forward," "regular," and "championship" tees distinguished by red, white, and blue markers respectively.

The *putting green* is a beautifully manicured area with a hole in which a flag at least 7 feet in height is placed to identify the cup (hole). The player uses the putter on this surface. Each hole may also have trees and shrubs or even an **out of bounds** defining where play is prohibited.

The *woods* are used from the teeing area (except on shorter holes where an *iron* would be used). The woods are used for distance. The irons are clubs for accuracy and are used to get to the green from the fairway or rough. The *putter* is used on the green or when just off the surface of the green. The length of the hole and playing ability of the player will also dictate the clubs used.

The *par* of each hole is the standard of scoring for each hole and is expressed in numbers such as a par 3, par 4, or par 5 or a par 72 course. Par is computed on a number of factors, the most important of which is distance. The very good player should be able to reach the green on a par 3 in one shot and two putts, reach the green on a par 4 in two shots and two putts, and on a par 5 in three shots with two putts. Holes vary in length. A par 3 is a short hole with distances of up to 250 yards for men and 210 yards for women. A par 4 is a medium length hole with distances of 251 to 470 yards for men and 211 to 400 yards for women. A par 5 is the longest hole, 471 yards and over for men and 401 and over for women. A score one under the par is a birdie and two under the par is an eagle. A score of one over the par is a bogey and two over par is double bogey. Naturally the best round (18 holes) is the lowest score.

RULES

The rules are simple: the golfer must play the ball as it lies and play the course as it is found. An explanation on how to use the rules book can be found inside the front cover of an official rules book. In almost all other sports the rules are imposed by an official; however, in golf your conscience is the umpire. It is left to the individual to know and abide by the rules. It is important for golfers to become familiar with the golf rules book and carry it in their golf bags at all times. The best way to learn both rules and etiquette is by either observing, or better still, playing with an experienced player. You should be familiar with the rules for play before you go out on the course. Knowing the rules may help you save strokes. Knowledge of the rules also allows you to penalize yourself in the appropriate manner in certain situations.

PENALTIES

Appendix B, "Rules simplified," gives a general overview of the rules from tee to green. There are thirty-four basic recognized rules of golf; each rule has definitions and qualifications together with penalties incurred if the rule is infringed. The following are the most common rulings on possible infringements and penalties incurred: no penalty, one-stroke penalty, two-stroke penalty, and disqualification.

► **Out of Bounds**
Ground on which play is prohibited. This area is marked by white stakes. You may not play from areas that are out of bounds.

▶ **No Penalty**

In certain situations you may obtain relief without incurring a penalty. In the following situations the ball may be lifted, cleaned, and dropped within one club length of the nearest point of relief without penalty:
1. A ball in casual water
2. A ball in ground under repair
3. A ball lying against staked trees or shrubs
4. A ball lying against a sprinkler head
5. A ball embedded in its own pitch mark
6. A ball landing on the wrong putting green
7. A ball on a cart path

How to drop a ball: The player, standing erect, holds the ball at shoulder height and arm length and drops it (see figure 4-3). See Rule 20-2 in *Rules Book*.

▶ **One-Stroke Penalty**

A one-stroke penalty is incurred and must be added to the score in the following situations:
1. A ball in play is moved after address. This is a one-stroke penalty and the ball must be replaced to the original position.
2. When a ball is lost or hit out of bounds.

FIGURE 4-3 In some situations you are allowed to obtain relief without a penalty by dropping a ball from shoulder height at arm length.

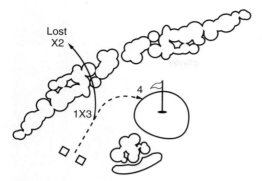

FIGURE 4-4 If you don't find a ball within five minutes you must penalize yourself one stroke and return to where the original ball was played.

A. Lost ball: if the ball is NOT found within five minutes (time allowed to search), you must penalize yourself one stroke and return to where the original ball was played. You are now penalized a stroke and distance (see figure 4-4).

B. A ball is out of bounds if it lies on ground on which play is prohibited. This area is marked with white stakes or white lines. If the ball was hit from the tee, you must return to the tee, where you may retee the ball and penalize yourself one stroke. You are now hit-

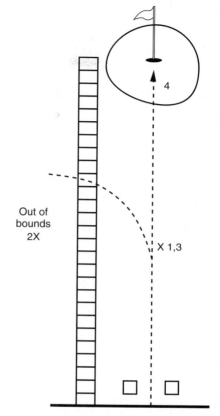

FIGURE 4-5 If a shot hit from the fairway goes out of bounds you must count the stroke, add a penalty stroke, and resume play from the position of the ball in the fairway before you hit your out-of-bounds shot.

ting shot number three. If the drive landed in the fairway and the next shot was hit out of bounds, you must drop the ball in the position from which you hit the ball out of bounds under penalty of one stroke. You must count the ball that went out of bounds (see figure 4-5). You are now playing stroke number four.

3. Unplayable lie. If the ball lies in a position from where it is impossible to hit or may cause injury, such as against a tree or lying on a rock or against the out of bounds fence, you may take relief. You may declare the ball unplayable (see figure 4-6) anywhere on the course except in a water hazard. The player is the judge as to whether the ball is unplayable. There are three options for relief under penalty of one stroke: (1) go back to the spot from where the ball was last played, (2) play the ball from within two club

FIGURE 4-6 The golfer is the judge as to whether the ball is unplayable. Calling a ball unplayable incurs a one-stroke penalty.

lengths of the unplayable point but not nearer the hole (if the unplayable ball is in a bunker, the ball must be dropped in the bunker with this option), and (3) go back as far as you wish on a line keeping the unplayable point where the ball lay between you and the hole (if the unplayable ball is in a bunker the ball must be dropped in the bunker with this option).

4. A water hazard. A water hazard is marked by yellow stakes or yellow lines and runs directly across the fairway. If the ball lands in a water hazard, the options are (1) play the ball as it lies (without penalty), (2) go back to the original spot and play another ball (one-stroke penalty) (see figure 4-7), or (3) go back as far as you wish on a line keeping the point of entry into the hazard between you and the flag (one-stroke penalty).

5. Lateral hazard. A lateral hazard is marked by red stakes or red lines and runs parallel to the fairway. The player's options are to (1) play the ball as it lies without penalty; (2) go back to the original spot, play another ball, and penalize yourself one stroke (you are now playing stroke three); (3) drop a ball within two club lengths of the point of entry (not nearer the hole) into the hazard (one-stroke penalty, now playing stroke three); (4) drop a ball within two club lengths on the opposite side of the hazard from the point of entry into the hazard (one-stroke penalty, now playing stroke three; and (5) go back on a line keeping the point of entry into the hazard between you and the hole and play the ball anywhere along that line under penalty of one stroke (this option may not be available if it is impossible to get to the far side of the hazard) (see figure 4-8).

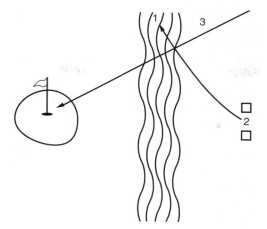

FIGURE 4-7 Options for play from a water hazard: **1**, play the ball as it lies; **2**, go back to the original spot and play another ball; or **3**, go back as far as you wish on a line keeping the point of entry into the hazard between you and the flag. Note: Options B and C incur a one-stroke penalty.

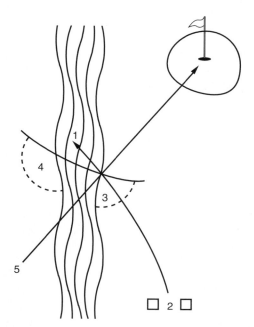

FIGURE 4-8 Options for play from a lateral hazard: **1**, play the ball as it lies with no penalty; **2**, go back to the original spot and play another ball; **3**, drop a ball within two club lengths of the point of entry (not nearer the hole); **4**, drop a ball within two club lengths on the opposite side of the hazard from the point of entry; or **5**, go back on a line keeping the point of entry into the hazard between you and the hole and play the ball anywhere along that line. Options 2, 3, 4, and 5 incur penalty of one-stroke.

6. Whiff or fresh air. If you swing with the intention of striking the ball and miss it, this is considered a stroke. Be sure to count it.

▶ Two-Stroke Penalty

Two-stroke penalties are incurred in the following situations:
1. While on the putting green, you putt and the ball strikes another ball. The penalty is two strokes (no penalty in match play). Play your ball as it lies and replace opponent's ball to its original position. When putting always have other players mark their balls on the green by placing a ball marker behind the ball (see figure 4-9). If you strike the flag when on the putting green it is also a two-stroke penalty. Always ask for the flag to be attended. If the flag is removed from the hole, do not leave it in the vicinity of the line of putt.
2. Improving lie. If a player attempts to improve the lie of the ball, it is a two-stroke penalty. For example, the ball is in the rough and the player steps behind the ball to flatten the grass.
3. Grounding the club in a hazard. The sole of the club must be kept above the ground. You may not touch the ground at address or during the backswing.

FIGURE 4-9 To avoid a possible two-stroke penalty ask other players to mark their balls on the green by placing a ball marker behind their ball.

4. Playing the wrong ball. A two-stroke penalty is incurred and the error must be corrected before teeing off at the next hole. Strokes played with the wrong ball will not count. Count the strokes played with the original, go back to that spot, and continue to play from there, adding a two-stroke penalty. In match play loss of hole will result.
5. Playing from outside the marked teeing ground. You must correct the error and play from within the teeing area. In match play the opponent may request you to cancel the stroke and play a ball from within playing area without penalty.

▶ Disqualification

In certain situations a player may be disqualified.
1. Practicing anywhere on the competition course on the day of stroke play competition.
2. Playing the wrong ball and not rectifying the situation before playing the next hole.
3. Playing from the wrong teeing ground and not rectifying it.
4. Failing to sign the score card or the marker's signature is omitted.
5. Signing an incorrect or incomplete scorecard.
6. Receiving advice from persons other than your caddy.

The rules that apply in certain situations may differ from stroke play to match play. If you are unsure of a decision, apply Rule 3-3 in *Rules Book:* Doubt as to Procedure. In stroke play put a second ball into play if you are doubtful of your rights or procedure. Announce to your fellow competitor your decision to use this rule and which ball you will count if the rules permit.

There may also be different rules for winter conditions. Players may be allowed to place the ball in the fairway or through the green (all areas on the course except teeing ground and putting green of hole being played and all hazards on the course). Check the local rules of the course. All players must play by the rules; it is not possible to cover all rules in this short section. Please carry, consult, and study your rules book. Check Appendix B, "Rules Simplified. "

HANDICAP

Handicaps were generally figured as seven eighths of the average of twenty rounds of golf. In today's highly technologic world, computer programs instantly compute handicaps and an individual's own index. When traveling and competing at another course, the United States Golf Association (USGA) slope and index

▶ Handicap
A method used to equate the different abilities of players. Handicap indexes are used to equalize players.

rating system based on the degree of difficulty of each course gives a quick computer adjustment up or down on the handicap. The result is that all handicaps are treated equally on any particular course.

For an example, a person with a 13 handicap and a 13.5 index may receive a 15 or even 12 handicap when computer adjustments are made at courses that vary in difficulty. For handicap information consult the club professional.

COMPETITION

There are two types of competition. One is called *stroke play* or *medal play* and the second is *match play*. With stroke play and medal play all the strokes for 18 holes (every putt must be holed out) are totaled, which gives the gross score. Subtract the handicap from the gross score to get the net score. The net score is used for competition. If a player with a 25 handicap scores 100 for 18 holes, the gross score is 100 and the net score is 75.

In match play each hole is a separate competition. The winner is determined by who wins the greatest number of holes. The players play a hole-by-hole competition and are not concerned about the total score for the 18 holes. This is a match between two players, unlike stroke play where all players compete against one another. In match play the lowest score on each hole wins that hole. Presuming that the two players have handicaps of 25 and 5, for the competition to be fair, the lower handicap must allow or give shots to the higher handicap (25). The number of shots allowed in match play is three-fourths the difference between their handicaps. For example, the player with the handicap of 25 would be allowed 15 shots. On 15 holes on the course the 25 handicap player subtracts one stroke from the actual score for match purposes. The score for the match should be called out after every hole. The terms *up, down,* and *all square* are used in match play. A player who is 2 up has won two holes more than the opponent. A player who is 2 down has lost two more holes than the opponent. If the score is "all square" the players have won, lost, or halved (same score on a hole) an equal number of holes.

Which holes the handicapped player receives shots depends on the course. Refer to the handicap column on the score card. If the player is allowed 15 shots, these shots will be received on holes where the handicap or index is 15 or less. On the scorecard (see figure 4-10), the shots would be allowed for a man at the following holes: 1, 3, 4, 5, 6, 7, 8, 9, 11, 12, 13, 14, 15, 16, and 18. A woman would receive strokes at holes: 1, 2, 3, 5, 6, 7, 8, 9, 11, 12, 13, 14, 15, 16, and 18.

Many types of competition may be played with the match play and stroke play format. The official name used for two people playing is *singles*. A *threesome* is used when three players play a round. The terms *foursome* or *fourball* are used for four players. When two players use one ball and play alternate shots it is called a Scotch foursome. When two players play their own balls and count the best ball for each hole, it is called a fourball. A golfer playing alone has no standing on the golf course and should call players behind through at all times.

HOLE NO.		1	2	3	4	5	6	7	8	9	Out		10	11	12	13	14	15	16	17	18	In	Total	HDCP	Net
GOLD	☐	291	175	360	211	387	343	399	520	524	3210		144	512	409	490	387	378	361	149	374	3204	6414		
WHITE	☐	278	161	315	200	371	327	383	506	509	3050	Player	131	503	359	473	364	366	347	136	364	3043	6093		
MEN'S HDCP		15	17	13	9	1	11	3	5	7			16	8	4	6	2	10	12	18	14				
PAR		4	3	4	3	4	4	4	5	5	36		3	5	4	5	4	4	4	3	4	36	72		
RED	☐	267	147	305	139	292	315	342	468	434	2709		118	426	301	411	338	294	339	120	356	2703	5412		
WOMEN'S HDCP		13	15	7	17	11	9	5	1	3			18	2	12	4	6	14	10	16	8				

Slope Rating: Red-113   Course Rating: Red-69.9

DATE   SCORER   ATTEST

FIGURE 4-10 Sample scorecard.

ETIQUETTE

In addition to the rules of "legal play" in golf, there are rules of etiquette that are equally important. Like the USGA rules, these are very important, but there is no penalty for breaking a rule of etiquette. Rules of etiquette must be attended to with respect.

The following guidelines should be used:

1. Be courteous on the course at all times. Have respect for yourself, other golfers, golf equipment, and the golf course.
2. Play the ball as it lies, and leave the course as you found it, in beautiful condition. No litter please!
3. Never make unnecessary noise or distract other players.
4. On the first tee the player with the lowest handicap has the **honor.** Thereafter, the lowest score from the previous hole is entitled to the honor.
5. Do not take practice swings on the tee box.
6. Always replace divots.

▶ **Honor**

The right to tee off first on any given hole. The player who scored the lowest on the preceding hole gets the honor.

7. Do not stand in a position that will distract other players or cause an accident. Position yourself correctly. Always stand face to face, and be aware of all golfers in the group.
8. Never move ahead unless all golfers have hit.
9. The player farthest from the hole plays first, and *away* is the term used to imply this.
10. Be aware of slow play at all times. Players in the group behind should not have to stand and wait for every shot. If there is a free hole ahead of you, call them through. Just move to the side and wave them through; allow them to finish on the green before you play your next shot.
11. Do not push the group ahead of you by hitting your ball into them. Give them time to play their shots and move ahead.
12. If you lose a ball and intend to use the five minutes allowed to find it, please call the group behind through if there is a free hole ahead.
13. Shout "fore" if any player is in danger of getting struck by the ball. This is a warning cry to the people ahead.
14. If the ball lands in a bunker, always rake the bunker after executing your shot.
15. If the approach shot to the green leaves any *plug marks,* which are ball depressions on the green, please repair them. Insert the pitch repair tool into the ground and lift the soil gently (see figure 4-11). Tap the grass gently with

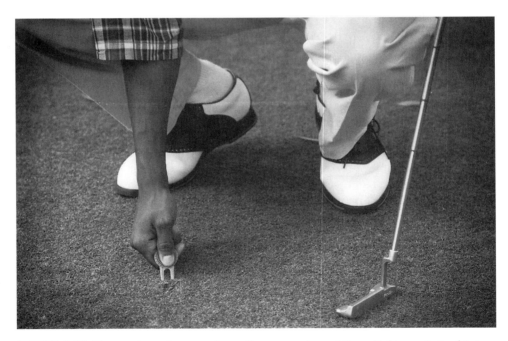

FIGURE 4-11 To repair a plug mark on the green, insert the pitch repair tool into the ground and lift the soil gently then tap the grass gently with the putter head. You may repair plug marks in the line of your putt without penalty.

Performance Tip

REMEMBER: PLAY SAFE AND SPEED UP PLAY!

the putter head. You may repair plug marks in the line of your putt without penalty. *Spike marks* in the line of your putt may not be repaired. These are caused by accidently dragging the cleats along the surface of the green. Always repair a spike mark when leaving the green.

16. Mark your ball on the green if it is on the line of the putt of another player. This can be done by placing a marker or a coin behind the ball and then lifting the ball. Replace the ball before lifting the marker.
17. Stand out of the line and the sight of another player who is putting and never stand behind the hole.
18. Walk behind the ball of another player. Do not walk on the line between the ball and the hole.
19. The player whose ball is closest to the flag will attend the flag. The player will hold the flag in the hole while the other player is putting and pull it from the hole when the ball is approaching. The flag is held for the player to see the hole clearly. When the flag is removed, place it on the ground out of sight and away from the putting line of the other players. Place the flagstick on the ground; do not throw it.
20. Replace the flag before leaving the green.
21. Leave the green only when all players have holed out.
22. Golf bags and carts should not be left on the green. Place these on the side of the green closest to the next tee and away from the **apron.**
23. Move to the next teeing area immediately. Do not stop to mark cards. This may be done while getting ready to tee off at the next hole.

SAFETY

Safety must be given special attention on the course, at the driving range, and anywhere else you may practice.

▶ **Apron**
The grass area surrounding the putting green. Also called the "fringe."

WEATHER

If there are signs of an impending storm, be careful and continue to observe the sky. Suspend play if there is lightning; usually there are three short sounds from the siren to discontinue play. You do not need to wait for this. Leave the course and go back to the clubhouse. Do not seek shelter under trees or use a steel-shafted umbrella.

In hot, humid weather precautions should be taken to avoid heat stroke. Wear a visor or hat and cotton clothing for absorption of perspiration. Drink plenty of water.

In wet weather appropriate footwear should be worn. Spikes or cleats are necessary for good footing. Club grips and hands must be kept dry to avoid a flying club, which could cause injury.

SAFETY ON THE DRIVING RANGE

Remember the following safety rules on the driving range:
1. Be aware of golfers on either side of you. Remain in your own hitting station.
2. Do not hit from out in front or from behind another golfer.
3. Do not retrieve tees or balls from a few feet in front of the line. Wait until "time out" is called to retrieve.
4. When chipping to the putting green, do not chip while students are on the green or fellow golfers are chipping from the opposite side of the green.

SAFETY ON THE COURSE

Remember the following safety rules on golf courses:
1. Call "fore" if any person is in danger of being hit by a club or ball. If you hear "fore," cover your head, turn your back, and duck.
2. Use personal space for practice swings; that is, only take a full swing if the area in the immediate vicinity is clear.
3. Stand so that you are facing players who are hitting and stay well out of their range.
4. If the ball lands in another fairway be conscious of oncoming players. These players have the right of way.
5. If the ball lands in trees or near a tree, check whether you can take a full swing. You could injure yourself by striking a branch or tree trunk on your backswing or follow through. Also, check for roots or rocks, which could cause injury or break a wrist. In addition, watch for balls deflecting from trees and changing direction.
6. If operating a golf cart, follow all safety procedures. DO NOT OPERATE A GOLF CART WHILE YOU ARE UNDER THE INFLUENCE OF

ALCOHOL. Do not operate the cart in an irresponsible manner. Always apply the foot brake, and set the parking brake when the cart is stationary.

7. If practicing indoors, be aware that the club and the ball can cause injuries, especially injuries to the eyes and head. Use soft or plastic balls. Use mats in each hitting station and adapt appropriate spacing between each mat. Remember that a call of "time out" means STOP. Do not hesitate to use this method to draw the attention of your fellow golfers.

TERMINOLOGY

All students must understand the terms used in golf. Consult Section 11 in your rules book, which covers definitions. Also, refer to Appendix A in this book (Golf Terms).

SUMMARY

- The game of golf is played on a course of 9 or 18 holes, and the main objective of the game is to get the ball into each hole in as few shots as possible.
- Each hole on a golf course consists of a teeing ground, a fairway, a rough, hazards, and a putting green.
- The par of each hole is the standard of scoring for each hole and is expressed in numbers such as a par 3, par 4, or par 5.
- A knowledge of the rules and etiquette of golf is essential to good play.
- Penalties for infringement of the rules of golf can include a one-stroke penalty, a two-stroke penalty, and even disqualification from the game.
- Types of competition in golf include stroke play and match play.
- Rules of etiquette and safety must be followed closely on the golf course.

THE **PERFECT SWING:**
SKILLS

OBJECTIVES

After reading this chapter, you should be able to do the following:

- Practice the full swing comfortably.
- Understand the laws, principles, and preferences of the swing.
- Describe how grip, setup, alignment, and ball placement affect the swing.
- Follow a simple practice routine.

KEY TERMS

While reading this chapter, you will become familiar with the following terms:

▶ Align/aim
▶ Downswing
▶ Follow-through
▶ Grip

▶ Hook
▶ Setup
▶ Slice
▶ Takeaway

PERFECT SWING

TWENTY-FIVE REPETITION METHOD OF LEARNING THE SWING

Before I address the strokes that are the bread and butter of this book, let me share my method for faster and more positive results. Begin learning the putting stroke with the ball, and continue to learn the short game with the ball while the full swing is introduced without the ball. To explain further, on day 1 begin on the putting green, learning grip, stance, alignment, and stroke. On day 2 continue on the putting green, but also learn the grip for the full swing; use the 7 iron for this practice. Grip and regrip the club twenty-five times. On day 3 begin chipping with the ball but introduce setup, stance, and alignment for the full swing, without the ball. Continue to practice the grip, setup, stance, and alignment for a number of days; practice without the ball and repeat twenty-five times. Continue this process until the pitch shot has been achieved with the ball. The full swing should feel comfortable once you have incorporated the **takeaway,** the **downswing,** and the **follow-through.** You have used the same process and have followed the routine of twenty-five repetitions in each area. Before even striking a golf ball with a mid iron or wood you should feel comfortable with the full swing. You now look like a golfer, achieved without the added pressure of incorporating all the concepts of the full swing in one session. Now you are ready to introduce a ball; your confidence should be high because you already have mastered putting, chipping, and pitching skills. You should also feel comfortable with the mechanics of the full swing.

IS THERE A PERFECT SWING?

There are a number of theories about what influences the golf swing. Dr. Gary Wiren developed a teaching model and explains that certain physical forces influence the swing and ball flight. Certain mechanical aspects within the swing

► **Takeaway**
The part of the swing that involves taking the club away from the ball to complete the backswing.

► **Downswing**
The part of the swing that involves swinging the club from the top of the backswing down through the ball.

► **Follow-through**
The part of the swing that involves swinging the club down the target line and holding the finish.

relate to these physical forces. All golfers make different choices that have a positive effect on the physical forces and mechanics. Dr. Wiren's model is known as the laws, principles, and preferences of golf.

The first priority is the laws. These are invariable and influence the flight of the ball. The second priority is the principles. Principles refer specifically to the golf swing and have a direct relation and influence on the laws. The grip, which is a principle, has a direct relationship on the club face. The last priority is preference. Preferences are limitless, a choice you make to interact the laws and principles. The choice of grip you use, whether it is overlap, interlock, or ten-finger; the position of feet on the ground; and the width of the stance can all have an influence on the swing. Preference is what feels good to you and works well.

LAWS

There are five ball flight laws that determine the flight of the ball.
1. Speed. The speed at which the club head moves through impact affects the distance a ball goes. The more acceleration through the ball, the greater the distance.
2. Path. The path that the club head takes through impact determines the initial direction of the ball. (The ball may then fly right or left because of an error in the club face position).
3. Face. Face may affect the final direction. If the face is open, the heel hits first; if it is closed, the toe hits first and a side spin is put on the ball. If the club face is open, a **slice** occurs, and if the club face is closed, a **hook** occurs. Open face at impact is when the club face is open to the target line and the ball travels from left to right (for right-handed golfers). This results in a slice. Closed face at impact is when the club face is closed to the target line. The ball travels from right to left (for right-handed golfers). This results in a hook. When the club face is square the ball flight should be straight provided the setup and alignment are correct. When the club face is open or closed ball flight is affected (see figure 5-1).

Performance Tip

Troubleshooting When Your Swing Is Hooking or Slicing

Check
1. Your grip
2. Your club face (leading edge should be square to target)
3. Alignment (body position in relation to target)

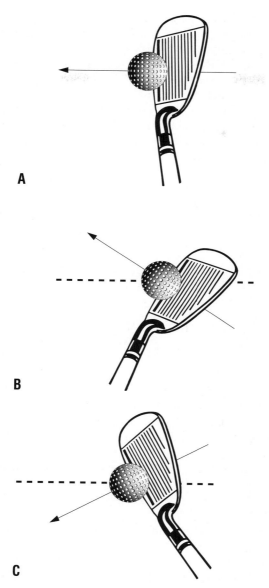

FIGURE 5-1 The face of the club at contact with the ball affects the ball's final direction. **A,** square-face contact should result in a relatively straight path. **B,** an open-club face results in a slice. **C,** closed-face contact will cause the ball to hook.

▶ **Slice**

A ball that flies drastically from left to right (from right to left for the left-hander).

▶ **Hook**

A ball that flies drastically from right to left (from left to right for the left-hander).

4. Angle of attack. Angle of attack determines both distance and trajectory. The angle of the golf club as it makes impact with the ball affects the trajectory and the distance the ball will fly. If the club strikes the ball below the center or equator of the ball, it will fly higher; if struck above the center or equator, it will fly lower.

5. Squareness of contact. An optimal position on the face of the club to strike the ball is referred to as the "sweet spot." The closer you strike the ball toward the sweet spot, the more solid the contact. When struck toward the center of the club face, the result is greater distance and direction. A ball hit toward the heel or the toe of the club face will result in loss of both distance and direction.

ERROR DETECTION

By understanding the laws, which are absolute, one can detect the error and make a correction.

PRINCIPLES

Principles are parts of the swing necessary for good results. The principles of the swing affect the laws. There are preswing and inswing principles.

▶ Preswing Principles

Grip. The grip has the greatest effect on the club face. The position of the hands on the club is most important. Ball flight will be affected by moving the hands to the right or the left on the club. A grip that is too tight or too loose will also affect the result.

Align/Aim. Align the body and the club face. The body, feet, hips, and shoulders should be parallel to the target line. The club face leading edge is square to the target.

Setup.
- Position of the feet: on the ground shoulder width apart, the weight toward the balls of the feet.
- The posture is relaxed; bend or tilt at the hips and allow the arms to hang freely.
- Position of the body: the position in relation to the ball, whether it is close or far from the ball.
- Position of the ball: place the ball forward, center, or back in the stance (depends on shot).

All preswing principles will have an effect on the consistency of the golf swing.

▶ Inswing Principles

Dr. Gary Wiren states that there are at least nine inswing principles.

Plane. The plane is the path on which the club is swung back and forward through the ball. Some players have a flat plane and others an upright plane, determined by build and distance from the ball at setup.

Width of Arc.   The width of the swing's arc will affect the distance the ball travels. The target arm must be extended; if this arm collapses, club head speed is lost.

Length of Arc.   The length of the swing's arc will also affect distance. The length relates to the back and through swing. The golfer should make a full shoulder turn with the club parallel to the ground.

Position of Target Wrist.   Note the position of the target wrist at the top of the backswing. The position is square, open, or closed. The square, or flat, position is most appropriate. The position of hands on club at address will ultimately determine position of target hand at top of the backswing.

Two-Lever Action.   A one- or two-lever action may be used. The one-lever action is used in chipping where the club and arms act as one and there is no wrist break. The two-lever system transmits greater force and thus more distance. The two-lever system is achieved by incorporating a wrist cock into the backswing.

Release.   The hands and forearms rotate through impact. For release to occur, muscular tension must be minimal. Tension may be the cause of the slice problem, due from lack of release. Once you have wrist cock in the backswing, you must release the hands and forearms at impact and through the ball. Acceleration through impact is only possible by releasing the hands and forearms.

Timing.   Timing is fusing all separate motions that make the swing. The club head, hands, hips, and rear shoulder must all work in sequence. Turning and returning to the ball in sequence produces perfect timing. The backswing is initiated with the upper body and the downswing with the hips, allowing the hands, rear shoulder, and club head to arrive together.

Dynamic Balance.   In all sports in which an object is propelled to a target, a transfer of weight is necessary. For example, a discus thrower needs the agility and balance of a ballerina. Field hockey players move into the ball and transfer weight to the forward foot. In golf the weight moves to rear heel and back to the target side. A smooth transition of weight is desired. You should remain in the posture of the setup throughout the swing.

Swing Center.   Your "swing center" is at the top of your sternum or breast bone. Try to keep this area steady and the swing will be more efficient. The head may move somewhat on the takeaway, without causing problems, provided the head stays behind the ball at impact. The head and the sternum should be in the setup position at impact.

▶ **Grip**
The position of the hands on the club.

▶ **Align/aim**
The alignment of the body and club face in relation to the target.

▶ **Setup**
The basic golf position and posture at address.

PREFERENCES

Preferences are personal and varied. An example of a preference is the type of grip you wish to use. Your choice of grip, setup, and tempo must suit your personality. Combine your choices for the most efficient results.

Grip, setup, and alignment make sound preswing mechanics that will allow you to build a simple, repeatable swing. This will put you in a position to repetitively apply the club face squarely to the ball at impact.

▶ **Grip**

The grip may vary from putting through the full swing; the grip is the position of the hands on the club. Remember that the only contact you have with the ball is through the grip. The hands dictate how the face of the club is placed to the ball; they give you control over the club head as it passes through impact.

> **NOTE: Target side is the left side for right-handed golfers. Target side is the right side for left-handed golfers.**

It is essential that every golfer master a sound grip. Both hands must work as a unit. You must be able to place the hands naturally on the club. The way your hands hang at your side is termed the "natural" position. Place your hands in a natural position on the shaft, with the palms facing and the thumbs slightly inward. The target hand is placed on the club. Place the club diagonally across the hand in the palm and fingers. Fold the fingers over the grip of the club. The pressure should be felt in the last three fingers of the target hand. Looking down, you should see a "V" made by the thumb and index finger that points between the chin and the rear shoulder. You should also see two knuckles of the target hand (see figure 5-2). Place the rear hand on the club, allowing the thumb of the target hand to fit snugly into the lifeline of the rear hand. The index finger of the rear hand should be in the trigger position below the thumb. The "V" between the thumb and index finger on the rear hand should point between the chin and the rear shoulder. Remember, grip softly. Most players have too tight a grip and therefore lose feel. On a scale of 1 to 10, the tightest grip is a 10 and the lightest grip is a 1. Grip pressure for a soft grip should be a 5. Always check the grip for the two "Vs" pointing between the chin and the rear shoulder.

Performance Tip

Remember: A GOOD GRIP equals A SQUARE CLUB FACE equals SQUARE CONTACT WITH THE BALL.

FIGURE 5-2 To master a sound grip both hands must work as a unit.

FIGURE 5-3 The interlock grip.

FIGURE 5-4 The ten-finger grip is also known as the baseball grip.

The three accepted grips for the full swing are similar. The main difference is the position of the little finger of the rear hand on the club.

1. Interlock. In the interlock grip the target hand is on top and the rear hand is underneath with the thumb resting on the side of the shaft. When looking down at the grip, you should see two knuckles of the target hand. The index finger of the target hand interlocks with the little finger of the rear hand (see figure 5-3).

2. Ten-finger. The ten-finger grip is also known as the baseball grip. The index finger of the target hand and the little finger of the rear hand lie beside one another on the shaft. This grip is not as popular as the interlock or overlap grips (see figure 5-4).

FIGURE 5-5 The overlap grip is sometimes called the Vardon grip.

3. Overlap. The overlap grip is also known as the Vardon grip, after Harry Vardon. The little finger of the rear hand overlaps the first joint of the index finger of target hand (see figure 5-5).

Take time to learn the fundamentals of a proper grip. Playing golf is like building a house, with the grip as the foundation on which you build. A weak foundation spells disaster down the road, in both home construction and playing golf.

▶ **Setup**

The setup is the basic golf position and posture of the golfer at address. It includes the position of feet on the ground (stance), the feet shoulder width apart, the weight on the balls of the feet, the knees slightly flexed, a bend or tilt from the hips, bottom out, arms hanging freely from body, and chin up. To achieve this position, stand upright; tilt forward from the hips with the bottom out; and hang the arms naturally, keeping a slight flex in the knees. Feel the shoulders over the balls of the feet. Place the hands on the club with the appropriate grip, about one-quarter inch from the top (see figure 5-6).

Ball Placement for the Setup. After you look down the target line from behind the ball, stand to the side with the feet together. Put the club face behind the ball, align the face, and move the target foot and then the rear foot into a position shoulder width apart. For the longer clubs place the ball closer to the target heel in the stance and for shorter clubs in the center of the stance. As the clubs get longer, move the rear foot away from the ball for a wider stance. Your hands will be placed just opposite the inseam of the pants of the target leg. Ball position is critical; if the ball is too far back in the stance, the ball will be pushed (to the right for right-handed golfers and the reverse for left-handed golfers). If a ball is too far forward in the stance, the ball will be pulled (left for right-handed golfers and the reverse for left-handed golfers). Some recommend playing the ball opposite the target heel for all clubs, but this may not be effective for a weak golfer. Very athletic individuals with strong legs may be powerful enough to play all shots

FIGURE 5-6 Setup refers to the basic golf position for addressing the ball.

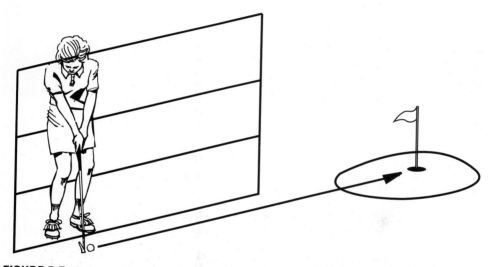

FIGURE 5-7 Proper alignment demands that all parts of the body—knees, hips, and shoulders—be on a line parallel with the target. The club head also needs to be squarely aimed at the target.

from a forward placement position. Most women and older players do better with the ball in the center of the stance. If this position does not suit, take some practice swings to identify the bottom of the swing and play the ball from that position.

▶ Alignment

Knees, hips, and shoulders should be on a line parallel with the target. The club head should be aimed at the target (see figure 5-7).

FIGURE 5-8 Addressing the ball involves taking your stance and setting up to the ball.

▶ Addressing the Ball

Taking your stance and setting up to the ball is called addressing the ball (see figure 5-8). In a hazard you may not ground the club when you address the ball.

PRACTICE

A perfect golf swing will not be achieved without hours of practice. Repetition of the swing will make you feel comfortable with it. Practice each of the preswing principles with whichever preference suits you best and adapt the twenty-five repetition method to your needs. As you feel comfortable in each area, add one more concept. You are well on your way to a lifetime of enjoyable golf without even striking a ball.

PLAN FOR PRACTICING THE PRESWING PRINCIPLES

1. Grip. Use twenty-five repetitions. Grip should be practiced on a daily basis, both on the driving range and at home. You could practice while watching

the television. Keep a grip handy, and while relaxing at home pick up the grip and continue to check and recheck the hand position.

2. Align/aim. Use twenty-five repetitions. Put clubs on the ground; these clubs should form a tunnel to the target. The ball is placed between the clubs. Coming from behind, take your stance with your feet, hips, and shoulders placed parallel to the nearer club. The club head is aimed at the target.

3. Setup. Use twenty-five repetitions. Move into the setup position, feeling relaxed. Check your posture in a mirror. Both the align/aim and setup may be practiced without a club and then with a club.

4. Takeaway. Use twenty-five repetitions. Move the club, hands, and arms away by turning the target shoulder away and behind the ball. Move the club head away from the ball close to the grass and concentrate on increasing the speed of the takeaway.

5. Hand position at the top of the backswing. Use twenty-five repetitions. Check the position of the target hand. It should be flat (see figure 9-10 for an example). Become comfortable with the use of a mirror for this practice.

6. Downswing. Initiate the downswing with the hips, allowing the hands, club, and rear shoulder to arrive together at impact.

7. Follow-through. Use twenty-five repetitions. Hold the follow-through position until the ball stops rolling. Use this method even if you did not get the ball airborne. You will promote the feeling of weight transfer and swing through and not at the ball.

Use the method of twenty-five repetitions, grip alignment, and swing into all concepts of your game. This type of learning reflects a pure form of specificity of training. The additional swings apparently enhance motor pattern and muscle recruitment.

SUMMARY

- A good method for mastering each aspect of a good golf swing is to practice by repeating each aspect of the swing—such as the grip—twenty-five times per day.
- A well-practiced full swing should feel comfortable and should incorporate the takeaway, the downswing, and the follow-through.
- The golf swing is affected not only by physical laws, but also by the player's application of the principles of the game and his or her personal preferences.
- The three accepted grips for the full swing are the interlock, the ten-finger, and the overlap.
- Practicing the preswing and inswing principles twenty-five times each will help develop a smooth, consistent swing.

Assessment 5-1

Checklist for Grip, Alignment, Setup, and Ball Position

Name _____   Section _____   Date _____

Use the following assessment checklist every time you practice to help you evaluate and improve your preswing skills.

> **NOTE: Target side is left side for right-handed golfers. Target side is right side for left-handed golfers.**

1. Grip
   _____ The Vs between the thumb and index finger of both hands are pointing between the chin and rear shoulder.
   _____ The hands do not feel too tight on the club.
2. Align/Aim
   _____ The feet, knees, hips, and shoulders are on a line parallel to the line of flight.
3. Setup
   _____ Feet are placed a shoulder width apart, and posture is relaxed.
   _____ Position of the body is standing tall with a slight tilt from the hips.
4. Position of the ball
   _____ The ball is placed in the center of the stance.
   _____ As the club gets longer, you are moving the ball forward in the stance.

CHAPTER 6

BASICS OF PUTTING: TECHNIQUE

OBJECTIVES

After reading this chapter, you should be able to do the following:

- Understand the importance of good putting in obtaining a respectable score.
- Repeat the same putting grip, setup, and stroke every time.
- Use a different technique for uphill, downhill, and sidehill putts.
- Recognize the importance of incorporating drills into practice.

KEY TERMS

While reading this chapter, you will become familiar with the following terms:

► Chipping

► Pitching

► Putting

► Regulation

THE SHORT GAME

The *short game* accounts for 63 percent of the game of golf and it should be given that amount of importance. The short game encompasses **putting, chipping,** and **pitching.**

PUTTING

If you begin your golf experience on the putting green, you will gain an immediate sense of accomplishment. Within a short time you will have achieved an adequate skill level to play stroke play and match play competition on the putting green. All good golfers are excellent putters. You may be able to hit the ball as long as Laura Davies, one of the longest hitters on the LPGA tour or Tiger Woods, on the PGA tour, but unless you can putt consistently with confidence, your score will never substantially improve. The majority of the population of golfers were not endowed with the athleticism of Davies or Woods. Fortunately putting is not about athleticism; it is about technique, feel, touch, and confidence. Technique and confidence can be achieved through practice. Seve Ballesteros, former U.S. Masters and British Open Champion is known for his magical and creative touch around the greens. Your score of 130 could very quickly become a 120 if you work to develop a little of your own magic and touch. If you are close to breaking a 100, 90, or 80 you should focus more on your putting. **Regulation** for putting is two strokes per hole. The quickest way to improve is practice. Your goal should be to make two and one putts consistently on every hole.

Putting is designed to be one-half of a total score. Par for putting on each hole is 2, or 36 putts in 18 holes. If you shoot 72 (par) for 18 holes, you should give putting that much importance in your practice.

KEEP IT SIMPLE

Putting is the most personal part of the golf game. Grip, stance, stroke, and ball position vary from individual to individual. Use the method that works for you whatever your grip, stance, or setup. My motto is " Keep it simple." The majority of the players on both the men and ladies tours use the *reverse overlap grip* shown in figure 6-1.

▶ **Putting**
Strokes made on the putting green to move the ball into the hole.

▶ **Chipping**
Strokes made from just off the green that have more roll than air time.

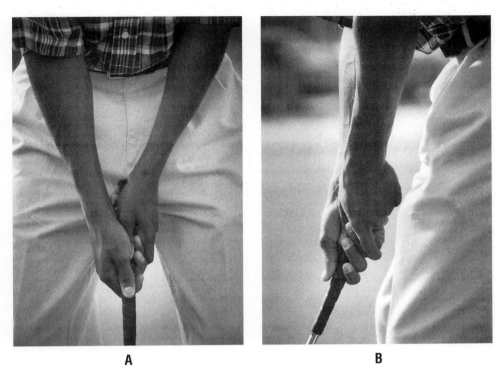

A   B

FIGURE 6-1 Reverse overlap grip. **A,** Front view. **B,** Side view.

With the palms facing, the target hand grips the club. The rear hand is placed on the club below the target hand. Place both thumbs down the front of the shaft. Place the index, or pointer, finger of the target hand over the fingers of the rear hand. Push the hands close together. The hands should be soft on the club in order to develop feel.

SETUP

The setup for putting is very personal and depends on your style. Any style is acceptable provided it allows you to square the putter face at impact and extend down the target line to the hole. The usual setup is to place the feet on the ground, shoulder width apart. Allow the weight to favor the target foot. Some players

---

▶ **Pitching**
Strokes executed with a lofted club, producing high trajectory and little roll.

▶ **Regulation**
Another term for par.

A   **B**

FIGURE 6-2 The set up. **A,** Facing. **B,** Down the line.

prefer to stand tall while others enjoy a slight knee flex. Place the ball forward of center in the stance. Keep your eyes over the ball. Figure 6-2 shows a good setup.

STROKE

The putting stroke is executed by swinging the club, arms, and shoulders. This is a pendulum action in which the hands, arms, and shoulders work as a unit. Do not use wrist action; breaking the wrists allows too much room for error and may cause the club to go off line. The feel for pendular action can be achieved by forming a triangle with the hands, arms, and shoulder. Swing back and through, keeping the club head close to the ground. Guide the club back and away from the ball with the target hand and use the nontarget hand or rear hand to accelerate through the ball. This creates the feel of rolling the ball. Accelerate through the ball. Some beginners make the error of taking the club back too far and then slow down coming into the ball. Your eyes should be over the ball, and the lower body should remain steady during the stroke. The amount of backswing is determined by the length of the putt. Take the club back and through the same distance. A longer putt requires a longer backswing and follow-through. Remember the laws developed

Performance Tip

Principles of Putting

Grip: Reverse overlap recommended, but not essential.

To Develop a Consistent Putting Stroke:

1. Pendulum action—arms/hands and shoulders work as one unit
2. Eyes over the ball; eyes and head remain steady
3. No lower body movement; keep the weight on the target side
4. Keep blade square; square the blade to a spot in front of the ball
5. Swing back and through on correct path or line to the hole
6. Place the ball forward of center in the stance—ball is struck slightly on the upswing
7. Putter always accelerates through the ball to the target
8. Concentrate on the feel of the swing and the impact with the ball

A Putting Checklist

1. Reverse Overlap Grip—Palms facing, thumbs down the shaft
2. Stance—Feet shoulder width apart, ball forward of center
3. Eyes over the ball
4. Pendulum action—arms, hands, and shoulders working as a unit. Keep blade close to the ground, and move the putter head back and through equal distance
5. No lower body movement
6. Feel—Develop this through practice

by Dr. Gary Wiren also apply to putting. In putting, speed, path, face, angle of attack, and squareness of contact are important, as demonstrated in figure 6-3.

PRESWING ROUTINE

As with all other golf strokes, you should have a preswing routine for putting. There are a number of methods for perfecting the preswing; when you become more familiar with the game you may introduce your own preswing routine. For the moment, make it simple.

1. Go behind the ball, either stand up or bend down low. Visualize a line between the ball and the hole.

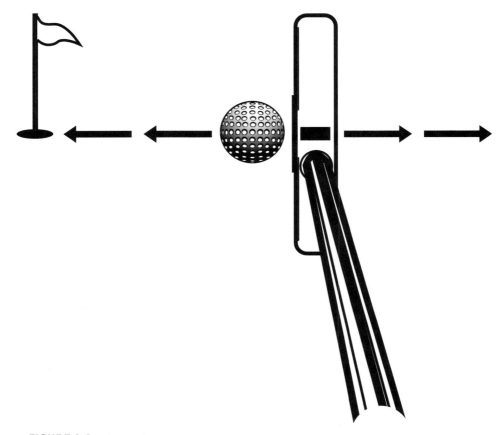

FIGURE 6-3 The club moves back and then through the ball toward the hole.

2. Pick a spot (on the ground) between the ball and the hole, a little in front of the ball. Move into the setup position, place the head of the club behind the ball, and square the face of the club with the spot in front of the ball. In short, setup, square the club face, visualize a line to the hole, visualize the ball dropping into the hole, and have a positive attitude.

READING THE GREEN

To perfect your putting game, you will need to learn to read the green. The more advanced player will check the putt from each side and in front and behind the hole. The green may have undulations, and the line of the putt to the hole may not be straight. The green may be fast or slow, the putt may be uphill or downhill. If the grass is shiny as one looks at it, the grass is growing away from you and the green will be fast. If the grass appears dull, the grass is growing towards you and the green will be slow. If the green is near water, the grass tends to grow towards the water, so the putt will run in that direction. If the green is near a mountain, usually the putt will run away from the mountain.

Performance Tip

Adjusting Your Putting Technique for Uphill, Downhill, and Sidehill Putts

Uphill putt:
Grip: Firmer
Ball placement: Toward the higher foot (target foot)
Stroke: Putt to an imaginary spot past the hole
Downhill putt:
Grip: Lighter
Ball placement: Toward the higher foot (rear foot)
Stroke: Place the ball toward the toe of the putter, putt to an imaginary spot just short of the hole, and the ball will drop into the hole.
Sidehill putt:
Grip: Normal
Ball placement: Forward of center
Stroke: When the ball is on the slope, play the ball to the high side of the hole. If the fall or slope to the right or left of the hole is very noticeable, check from behind the ball and pick a point along that line where the ball will fall to the hole. Square the blade to that point along an imaginary line to the hole.

Performance Tip

Remember:
Putt for distance; direction will come when control of distance is mastered. Think positive: Imagine how you will make the stroke rather than how you will miss the stroke.

PUTTING DRILLS

Drills and checklists can be used in a productive manner to assess and improve your golfing skills. Relying on practice time on the range alone is often damaging, especially when you continue to putt or hit balls without correcting the error. Use the appropriate drill and incorporate it into your program for best results.

Hint: When performing any of the following drills, it helps to keep three concepts in mind:
- Feel: Concentrate on the feel of the swing and the club's impact with the ball
- Roll: Focus on the sensation of rolling the ball gently forward
- Smooth: Try to make the motion of your swing as smooth as possible

IMPROVING YOUR PUTTING SETUP

Skill Development: Putting (Setup)
Levels: Beginner, Intermediate, Advanced
Start Position:
- Setup at ball
- Arms hanging freely
- Blade flat on ground
- Eyes over ball
- Balanced feel
- Have partner check setup position while looking down the target line and facing partner

Evaluation: You know you are improving when you feel comfortable over the ball and your partner no longer needs to make corrections in position of the feet, hips, shoulders, or the ball position.

PERFECTING THE PENDULUM MOTION AND SWING PATH

Skill Development: Putting (Pendulum motion and swing path)
Levels: Beginner, Intermediate, Advanced
Start Position:
- Place two clubs (railway track) on ground (see figure 6-4). Move putter back and forth between the clubs
- Move the putter back and through and back to the setup position
- Feel club, arms, and shoulders move as a unit
- Check to see if blade is square, swing back and through
- Back through and hold out in front
- Distance back equals distance through
- If head of putter makes contact with railway track on the ground, the stroke needs to be checked

FIGURE 6-4 Perfecting the pendulum motion and swing path takes repeated practice.

FIGURE 6-5 You will notice marked improvement when you can relate these swing lengths to distance.

Evaluation: The motion and the path is correct if the stroke can be executed smoothly without touching the track.

MASTERING DIFFERENT SWING LENGTHS

Skill Development: Putting (Swing length)
Feel difference in swing lengths (see figure 6-5)
Levels: Beginner, Intermediate, Advanced
Start Position: Setup beside a yardstick

FIGURE 6-6 The yardstick should be marked right and left of center 1″, 2″, and 3″.

The yardstick should have tape on it and should be marked right and left of center, 1″, 2″, 3″, 4″, and so on (see figure 6-6).

This board is good for teaching swing length.

- Practice strokes, 1″–1″
- Practice strokes, 2″–2″
- Practice strokes, 3″–3″

Note the results. Is there a difference in distance the ball travels? Be aware of stroke length and distance factor.

Evaluation: You have improved when you can relate the swing length to the distance.

THE ALTERNATE DRILL

Skill Development: Putting (Speed/direction)

Levels: Beginner, Intermediate, Advanced

Start Position: Use three balls, putt all three from the same spot to three different targets.

Evaluation: If your consistency of hitting the target improves with each rotation, you are improving. If the direction is inconsistent, place the ball between tracks on the ground, which form a tunnel to the target.

THE CIRCLE DRILL

Skill Development: Putting (Assertive short putts)
Levels: Beginner, Intermediate, Advanced
Start Position: Place six balls in a circle, one club length from the hole. Move from the right to the left putting each ball into the hole. Move left to right for the left-handed golfer.
Evaluation: You are improving when your success rate is increasing. Your goal is to succeed with all six balls. If you are inconsistent, concentrate on the feeling of getting the back of target hand finishing in the hole.

THE CLUSTER TECHNIQUE OF PUTTING PRACTICE

Skill Development: Putting (Feel length of putt)
Levels: Beginner, Intermediate, Advanced
Start Position: Setup as for a putt. Putt three to six balls in rapid succession looking only at the ball you are putting. The result should be three to six balls in a cluster. Practice the feel for different putt lengths. Emphasis: Feel for length of putts.
Evaluation: When two out of three or four out of six balls end in a cluster, you are improving.

THE LADDER DRILL

Skill Development: Putting (Swing length)
Levels: Beginner, Intermediate, Advanced
Start Position: Place clubs or tees on the green three feet apart. Use the distance between the clubs or tees as a guide to practice different length putts. Putt to the farthest tee first. Continue until you putt the last ball to the nearest tee.
Evaluation: As your success rate increases, you are improving. If you are inconsistent, practice the cluster drill again.

THE LINE DRILL

Skill Development: Putting (Compact stroke)
Levels: Beginner, Intermediate, Advanced

FIGURE 6-7 To develop a compact stroke putt closest to the hole first and continue until all balls have been holed out.

Start Position: Place four to six balls in a line four inches apart. Putt closest to the hole first and continue to putt until all balls are holed out (see figure 6-7). This helps to develop a compact stroke. This may also be adapted to the track.
Evaluation: Your goal is to hole out six putts. As you continue to practice the drill, if you hole out one more putt on each rotation, you are improving. If you notice inconsistency, try the yardstick drill again.

THE ONE-HAND DRILL

Skill Development: Putting (Pendulum action)
Levels: Beginner, Intermediate, Advanced
Start Position: Use the target hand only on the club. Make four to six putts; then use the nontarget hand on the club and repeat the drill. (Aware of pendulum action.)
Evaluation: You are improving when you feel more in control of the putter and the putts are ending up in the hole. You should have a firm wrist. If you find it difficult to retain a firm wrist try the shaft against arm drill.

THE "SPOKES OF THE WHEEL" DRILL

Skill Development: Putting (Distance/swing length)
Levels: Beginner, Intermediate, Advanced
Start Position: Stand in the center of the green as in the center of a wheel. Putt outward along different spokes to the fringe of the green. Use at least six balls.
Evaluation: You are improving when most of the balls stop before the fringe on each rotation. If the balls are consistently stopping short, concentrate on acceleration of the putter through the ball.

THE TEE DRILL

Skill Development: Putting (Distance and accuracy)
Levels: Beginner, Intermediate, Advanced
Start Position: Place a tee or a number of tees in the ground. Putt balls to the tees. This helps you concentrate on the stroke and speed. Beginning golfers become so hole-oriented they forget about speed. By using the tees, more emphasis is placed on feel and thus speed.
Evaluation: Your goal is for all the balls to surround the tee in the ground. You are improving when the balls end in a cluster around the tee. If you notice some inconsistency in length, concentrate on the stroke without the ball.

THE THREE SECOND DRILL

Skill Development: Putting (Feel for distance)
Levels: Beginner, Intermediate, Advanced
Start Position: Practice the stroke looking at the target only. When the feel for distance is good, make the putt looking at the ball only. After making practice strokes looking at the target, pick the appropriate one. You must now putt within three seconds.
Evaluation: When you can relate the appropriate practice swing to the distance, you are improving. If results are inconsistent, refer to the swing length of 1"–1" or 2"–2" drill.

THE TRACK DRILL

Skill Development: Putting (Club path)
Levels: Beginner, Intermediate, Advanced
Start Position: Use two clubs on the ground at the hole. Place each club parallel about a putter head apart. Place three or four balls between the track, and putt the ball nearest to the hole (as in figure 6-7). You may also use the track on the ground with longer putts.

Evaluation: When your swing is smooth and consistent and the club head never touches the track on the ground, you have improved. Your results should be each ball in the hole, provided the swing length is sufficient. If you do not improve, practice the swing without the club, concentrating on the pendulum action.

THE SHAFT AGAINST THE ARM DRILL

Skill Development: Putting (Eliminate active hands)
Levels: Beginner, Intermediate, Advanced
Start Position: Grip down the club. Place the shaft (butt end) against the target arm. If the grip end of the shaft moves away from the arm, the hands have been too wristy.
Evaluation: If the shaft remains against the target arm you have improved. Adapt your regular grip and stroke and incorporate a ball. If the wristy action continues, adapt the swing back and through and hold just ahead of the point of impact. Check for a firm wrist in the finish position.

A PROGRAM FOR PUTTING PRACTICE

Introduce the twenty-five repetition drill. Grip, align/aim, setup, and stroke.

To begin each practice session, use the rear (nontarget) hand to roll balls. This helps to enhance the feeling of rolling the putt. Introduce the putter. Use a number of the drills to make practice more interesting and to enhance the putting stroke. Before each putt adapt the putting routine. Practice long and short putts. Use the following as an example of a practice program.

1. Roll balls to targets.
2. Make long putts—cluster drill, use six balls. Repeat the practice six times. Introduce the alternate drill, using three different holes.
3. Putt with one hand on the club.
4. Short putts—use tracks on the ground (see figure 6-7). Feel the back of the target hand going into the hole.
5. Introduce competitions, alone or with a partner.
6. Practice indoors on the carpet.

Whatever practice routine you use, give your putting the importance it deserves. Putting should receive 50 percent of your time, considering that about 50 percent of your strokes in a round are putts. No one can teach you the concept of feel; this will only be achieved through hours of practice. Whatever method used is personal. Keep in mind that the goal is to putt the ball in the hole consistently.

SUMMARY

- The *short game,* which includes putting, chipping, and pitching, accounts for 63 percent of the game of golf and should be given great importance.
- All good golfers are excellent putters.
- Technique and confidence in putting can be achieved through practice.
- Par for putting is two strokes per hole.
- The reverse overlap grip is the grip most often used in putting.
- As with all other golf strokes, having a preswing routine for putting is very helpful.

Assessment 6-1

Putting Evaluation

Name _____   Section _____   Date _____

Until you feel very comfortable with your putting routine, use the following evaluations to test your putting skills and determine which areas you may still need to improve.

Record score for a 9-hole stroke play competition at the beginning of the term, and reevaluate on two more occasions. The par for the 9 holes is 18 strokes. You strive to better your own score. You are competing only with yourself. Record the scores (see table 6–1). Did you leave the first putt too short or too long, or was the error in the short putt area?

1. Work on your weaknesses.
2. Continue to practice your strengths.

Have you improved? Level par or under is your goal!

TABLE 6-1
Putting Evaluation

Hole	Par	1st Score	2nd Score	3rd Score
1	2			
2	2			
3	2			
4	2			
5	2			
6	2			
7	2			
8	2			
9	2			
Total	18			

Next to score indicate whether putt was long (L) or short (S) of hole or close enough for a tap in (T).

Sample:	Hole	Par	My Score
	1	2	2/T

CHAPTER 7

BASICS OF CHIPPING: TECHNIQUE

OBJECTIVES

After reading this chapter, you should be able to do the following:

- Know when to execute the chip shot.
- Understand the principles for executing the stroke.
- Demonstrate the ideal clubs to use for the chip shot.
- Understand that confidence can build success.
- Adapt drills for improvement.

KEY TERMS

While reading this chapter, you will become familiar with the following terms:

► **Chip Shot**

CHIPPING

The **chip shot** is used from just off the green. The goal is to get the ball close enough to the hole in order to tap in the putt. You should hit this shot with the intention of sinking the chip into the hole. Simple! Try approaching it as a putting stroke from just off the green. Building on the lessons in chapter 6, your chip shot will be an adaptation of the putting grip and pendulum stroke.

CLUB CHOICE

The club you choose is dependent on the terrain between you and the hole and how far the flag is from the edge of the green. Any club from a 5 iron to a sand wedge may be the correct choice. The chip shot has a low ball flight, landing on the edge of the green and rolling to the hole. If you use a 5, 6, or 7 iron, it is a chip with little air time and a long roll. Using an 8, 9, wedge, or sand wedge, will give you a chip with more air time and a shorter roll. The more lofted clubs are used when there is very little green between you and the flag. Use the club that will land the ball on the green and allow the ball to run to the hole. Let the club face lift the ball. The less loft the less air time. If you execute your putting stroke the loft on the club face will lift the ball. Do not try to scoop up the ball. Let the club head do the work (see figure 7-1).

THE STROKE

The chipping stroke is developed from the putting stroke, therefore, take your putter and make about six putting strokes from off the green; keep practicing until you putt a ball to the hole. Take a 7 iron and make the same stroke; the ball travels for a short time in the air. The reason is that the face of the 7 iron has more loft than the putter.

With the new club you need to make a few adjustments to your grip and stance. You should continue to use the reverse overlap grip and grip down the club, almost to the metal. Set your hands ahead of the ball. Your feet should be close together but slightly open. Do this by moving the target foot back a little. Place your hands high and move closer to the ball, with the ball towards the toe of the club for added control. The club face aims at the target, and the feet are aimed left

▶ **Chip Shot**
Used from just off the green, the aim is to get the ball close enough to the hole to tap in the putt.

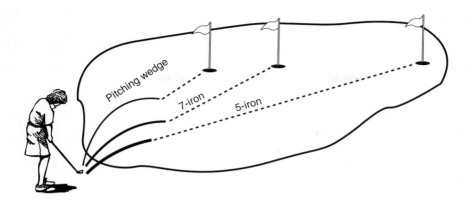

FIGURE 7-1 Chipping to the green.

of the target and slightly open (reverse for the left-handed golfer). Keep your shoulders square (parallel to the target line). The reason for this slightly open stance is that there is room for the hands to swing through and the hips are out of the way. Place your weight on the target foot and keep it there throughout the swing. Your weight should be ahead of the ball at address and throughout the swing. Be sure to keep your head over the target foot. Place the ball center or toward the forward foot in the stance, and square the club face to the ball. Make a pendulum stroke with the shoulders, arms, and club working as a unit. Keep the hands ahead of the ball at contact. Keep your target wrist firm throughout the stroke and through the finish. Brush the grass through the ball. Finish with the club low and close to the ground with the weight on the target side.

For longer chips, finish with the weight on the target side and the nontarget knee moving toward the target. If you allow the clubhead to pass the hands at impact, you will have weak shots, scooped or topped. Remember: *The stroke must be slow and firm.* Compare yourself to figure 7-2 for proper setup and execution of the chip shot. Your backswing needs to be longer and your stroke firmer the farther you are from the hole. If you are closer to the hole, use a shorter backswing and a little less pace. When there is a bunker or a slope and little green between you and the flag use, the more lofted 9 iron, pitching wedge, or sand wedge (see figure 7-3).

FIGURE 7-2 For proper execution the stroke must be slow and firm.

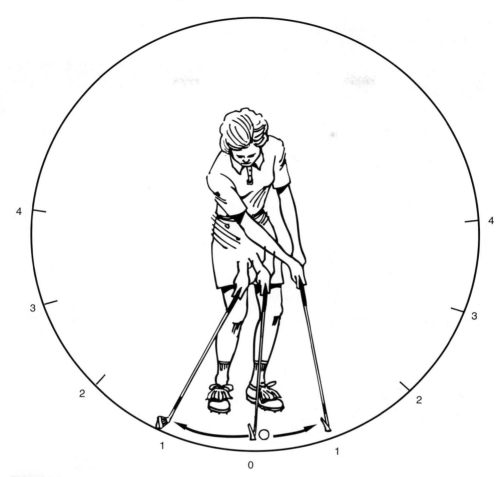

FIGURE 7-3 With continued practice you will be able to properly gauge the distance of your shot by the height of your swing.

CONFIDENCE

Whatever club you use, chipping, like putting, is about touch. The stroke is about feel and confidence. As you develop your own style, you will build confidence with hours of practice. With every chip shot your goal should be to hole it out (get the ball into the hole). If you are unsuccessful in sinking your shot, the ball should be as close to the hole as possible for a tap in. The more you see the ball going into the hole, the more confidence you build in your ability to succeed. Every time you approach the shot, visualize the ball traveling into the hole and chip it.

Performance Tip

Principles of Chipping

Grip: Use the Reverse Overlap as for Putting
(Please see figure 6-1 for an illustration of the reverse overlap grip.)

- Chip (low running shot) 5, 6, 7, 8, 9, PW, and SW
- Shortened grip (recommend reverse overlap)
- Grip to end of grip, with the hands high
- Arms, hands, and shoulders form a triangle with the hands ahead of the ball
- Smooth pendulum stroke (as putting)
- Narrow, open stance (please see figure 9-11 for an illustration of square, open and closed stances); shoulders remain square
- Knees and hips flexed
- Weight favors target side
- Position the ball center to forward in the stance, close to the toe of the club
- No lower body movement; keep weight on target side throughout the swing
- Keep the hands ahead of the ball at contact
- Swing back and through to target, 1 to 1 swing or 2 to 2 swing (one lever swing); swing the club back and forward an equal distance, accelerate through the ball

DRILLS

ACTIVE HANDS DRILL

Adapt the putting drills to chipping
Skill Development: Chipping (Active hands)
Level: Beginners
Start Position: Grip the club in the normal manner (for chipping). Extend the shaft of the club; use a broken shaft or another club. If the extended shaft hits the target side of the golfer on the follow through, the hands are too wristy.

FIGURE 7-4 The Active Hands Drill will let you know if your hands are too wristy and help you prevent problems with scooping the ball.

Firm the target wrist. Swing back and through; hold the finish position out in front (see figure 7-4).

As in the putting stroke if the target hand becomes too wristy and the golfer attempts to scoop the ball, there will be numerous problems.

Evaluation: If you continue to finish the swing out in front without the extended shaft hitting the target side, your stroke is improving. If you notice little improvement, use the putter from off the green to feel the stroke and then adapt the pendulum stroke with the chipping club.

CROSS LEGS AT ADDRESS

Skill Development: Chipping (Weight on the target side)
Levels: Beginner, Intermediate, Advanced
Start Position: Setup with the rear foot crossed over the target foot. This promotes a steady lower body and the feeling of the weight on the target side. Use pendulum stroke.
Evaluation: If you notice a crisp stroke at impact and the weight over the target foot with the ball rolling to the target, you have improved. If you continue to hit heavy behind the ball, you must adapt the drill until you can relate to the feeling of a steady lower body.

SETUP WITH TWO PARALLEL CLUBS ON THE GROUND

Skill Development: Chipping (Pendulum action/path)
Levels: Beginner, Intermediate
Start Position: Place the ball between the clubs (track), which point to the target. You may use different clubs for the execution of the stroke; note the distance covered with each club. Continue to use the pendulum action as for putting. The clubs on the ground are used as a guide for the back and through path (pendulum action).
Evaluation: Remove the track when you consistently roll the ball along the target line. The swing path is correct if while during your swing, there is no tendency to strike the track on the ground. If there is inconsistency in the direction, you must continue practicing. Place one club on the ground along the target line, and swing your club back and through over this club.

LADDER DRILL

Skill Development: Chipping (Swing length)
Levels: Beginner, Intermediate, Advanced
Start Position: Setup as for chipping; place clubs or tees on the green three feet apart. Chip to the farthest club or tee first and continue until you chip to the nearest club or tee.
Evaluation: You are improving when you are consistent. If you continue to be inconsistent, practice a swing length drill, 1 to 1 or 2 to 2.

Performance Tip

Checklist for Chipping

1. Grip down the rubber of shaft, use putting grip
2. Pendulum action
3. Narrow, slightly open stance; shoulders square
4. Keep weight on the target side
5. Place ball center to forward of center in the stance
6. Hips and knees flexed; get close to your work
7. Keep hands ahead of the ball at contact

TARGET DRILL

Skill Development: Chipping (Direction/speed)
Levels: Beginner, Intermediate, Advanced
Start Position: Setup three targets. Use twenty-one balls. Alternate between the short, medium, and long target.
Your goal is to place three balls within the leather at each target. You must alternate after every chip.
Evaluation: If the goal has not been achieved after twenty-one balls, check your swing length. Hands may also be too active; practice the extended shaft drill. You are improving when you have completed the task and have not used all twenty-one balls.
Many of the putting drills may be adapted for chipping.

PRACTICE

Introduce your practice of twenty-five repetitions, grip, align/aim, and setup. Here is an example of a practice program.
1. Toss balls at different targets using the rear hand. Toss underhanded with a stiff wrist. This creates feel. Good putting, chipping, and pitching are very dependent on feel and touch.
2. Introduce drills; maybe chip with legs crossed.
3. Chip with target hand only; chip with rear hand only.
4. Alternate long and short chips.
5. Place golf bag on the ground and chip over it.
6. Experiment with different clubs.
7. Chip and hold finish.
8. Feel that you can hole out every chip.
9. Learn to visualize each shot and stroke it into the hole. If you practice this area of the game it will change your scores dramatically.

SUMMARY

- The chip shot is used from just off the green with the goal of holing out.
- The drills and basics of putting can be easily adapted to improve your chip shot.
- Club choice depends on your distance from the hole and the lay of the terrain. A 5, 6, or 7 iron will give you little air time with a long roll and an 8 or 9 iron or wedge will give you more loft with a shorter roll.
- Keep your stroke slow and firm. Visualize the ball into the hole with every stroke.

Assessment 7-1

Chipping Evaluation

Name _____   Section _____   Date _____

Use the 9-hole chip and putt competition on a regular basis as you strive to better your score. The par for the 9 holes is 18 strokes. Your goal is to get up and down from off the green. Record your aces, your one over par (Par is 2), your chip errors, and your putting errors. Record the scores. Continue to reevaluate on a regular basis (see table 7-1). Work on your weaknesses. Continue to practice your strengths. Have you improved? Level par or under is your goal!

TABLE 7-1
Chipping Evaluation

Hole	Par	My Score	Chip L = Long S = Short G = Good	Putts
1	2			
2	2			
3	2			
4	2			
5	2			
6	2			
7	2			
8	2			
9	2			
Total	18			

CHAPTER 8

BASICS OF PITCHING: TECHNIQUE

OBJECTIVES

After reading this chapter, you should be able to do the following:

- Recognize how to determine the ideal approach shot.
- Learn the basics for the short pitch, the long pitch, and the pitch from long grass.
- Understand the principles of pitching.
- Decide which club is the appropriate choice for the pitch shot.
- Evaluate when the pitch shot should be executed.
- Understand the use of drills to help improve weaknesses in technique.

KEY TERMS

While reading this chapter, you will become familiar with the following terms:

▶ **Approach Shot**
▶ **Pitch Shot**

PITCH SHOT

After mastering the basics for chipping and pitching, the biggest problem facing the golfer is the number of choices in club and type of pitch. The **pitch shot** is an **approach shot.** Direction is important; the goal is to stop the ball as close as possible to the flag. The shot calls for a more lofted club than the club used for chipping. Make a pitch shot when the situation demands that you need more carry and less roll. The clubs of choice are a 9 iron, pitching wedge, sand wedge, or lob wedge. Many golfers carry more lofted wedges than the sand wedge to use exclusively for the pitch shot.

TYPE OF SHOT

If you are close to the green with an obstacle between you and the flag, use a short pitch. If you are farther away from the green, you need a pitch with more carry and less roll.

SHORT PITCH

Many fundamentals for pitching are similar to those adapted for chipping. The short pitch is used within twenty yards of the green and is the ideal shot to get over an obstacle.

CLUB AND GRIP

The short pitch demands the use of a sand wedge or a club with more loft. Grip the club using your choice of interlock, overlap, or ten-finger grip. Adjust the hands on the grip to make the grip weaker. Instead of seeing two knuckles on the target hand, move both hands toward the target until just one knuckle is visible. Grip down on the shaft with the top of the shaft pointing up toward you.

Experiment and practice until you find the approach that is most comfortable and provides consistent results.

▶ **Pitch Shot**
An approach shot with the goal of stopping the ball as close to the flag as possible.

▶ **Approach Shot**
A shot played to the putting green.

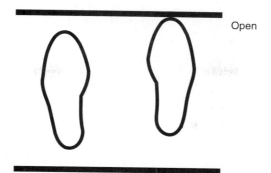

Open

FIGURE 8-1 While setting up the pitch shot you need to adapt an open stance with your target foot pulled slightly away from the line. Be sure to keep your hips and shoulders square.

SETUP

Stand close to the ball with your eyes directly over the ball. The position of your feet on the ground is slightly wider than for the chip shot. Adapt an open stance with the target foot moved away from the line (see figure 8-1). Keep your hips and shoulders square. Place the ball center or forward of center in the stance. By placing the ball back in the stance closer to the rear foot, the club comes into the ball at a steeper angle and the loft is taken off the face. Playing the ball forward of center in the stance creates a higher trajectory. Your body weight should favor the target side and remain there throughout the shot.

SWING

Use an arms and shoulder swing with no wrist break. Firm your target hand and keep it firm throughout the swing. This will minimize wrist action.

During the backswing your head and eyes need to remain steady over the ball. Look at the back of the ball throughout the swing. The backswing is longer than that required for the chip shot. Relax the shoulders and arms, and swing through the ball with a firm target wrist. The back of the target hand remains facing the target. The face of the club looks skyward. The finish position should enable you to hold a coin on the club face without the coin falling off. That is possible if the target wrist remains firm throughout the swing.

You should soften the target arm on your follow through, but your target wrist must remain firm. Keeping your eyes focused on the back of the ball is crucial for a successful short pitch (see figure 8-2).

FIGURE 8-2 Keeping your eyes focused on the back of the ball is essential for executing an accurate short pitch.

LONG PITCH

The long pitch shot is played farther from the green where more air time and less roll is required. The choice of club is dependent on the playing ability of the golfer and the distance from the target. The choice of club could be a 9 iron; pitching wedge; sand wedge; or one of the new specialty clubs, which have a greater degree of loft. Advanced golfers can play a long pitch with a pitching wedge from 100 yards out. This shot is an extension of the short pitch swing and a shorter version of the full swing.

GRIP

You will need to adapt your regular grip by using an overlap, interlock, or ten-finger grip. Grip lower on the shaft for shorter shots and grip at the top of the shaft for longer distances.

SETUP

To setup, use a slightly wider stance than that adapted for the short pitch. Bend or tilt from the hips with a slight knee flex. Square up your hips and shoulders keeping your shoulders level. Place the ball center or forward of center in the stance. Move your hands forward toward the target, slightly ahead of the ball.

FIGURE 8-3 The long pitch. **A,** Setup. **B,** Backswing. **C,** Contact. **D,** Follow-through.

Again, your weight will favor the target side. The open stance allows you freedom to swing without too much body movement.

SWING

The swing for the long pitch is easy but firm. It is an arms and shoulder swing; the rear elbow will hinge on the back swing. Keep the swing compact. A slight wrist break and weight transfer to the rear foot will occur because this swing is longer than usual. This will happen naturally as the swing becomes longer. Try to concentrate on swinging your shoulder and arms while keeping your wrists firm. This will eliminate unnecessary hand action. Take a compact backswing and allow the target arm to remain firm through impact, allowing the club face to stay square. Continue with the club head low and forward toward the target. You will need to minimize body movement. Your weight starts on the target side and although there is a slight weight shift, you should feel your knees driving toward the target on the follow through. Too much hand action will cause high and short shots (see figure 8-3).

Performance Tip

Principles of Pitching

- Narrow open stance
- Grip down on the shaft with the hands ahead of the ball
- Weight on the target side
- An arms and shoulder swing
- Compact swing
- Firm through and beyond impact
- Minimize the weight shift
- Weight on the target side at the finish

PITCHING FROM LONG GRASS

When pitching from long grass or the rough, place the ball toward the back of the stance to minimize the amount of grass between the club face and the ball. Too much grass between the club face and ball at impact will cause the ball to be pulled or fly left of the target (reverse for the left-handed golfer). Remember to swing through the ball.

PITCHING DRILLS

When the golfer progresses from chipping with a swing length of 1 to 1 and 2 to 2, increase the swing length for pitching. The backswing and forward swing will vary depending on the distance from the target. Being closer to the target necessitates a shorter swing, while being farther from the target will require a longer swing. (Refer to figure 7-3.)

ALTERNATE DRILL: HIT SHOTS ALTERNATELY TO EACH TARGET

Skill Development: Pitching (Distance and direction)
Levels: Beginner, Intermediate, Advanced

Start Position: Setup as for the pitch shot, play to short, medium and long targets. Alternate; never play two shots to the same target.
Evaluation: You are improving when you hit the targets consistently, and you can adjust the swing length for the appropriate distance. If you are missing the target on the right or left, revert to the clubs on the ground for the setup. If distance is the problem, revert to the swing length drill.

SWING LENGTH DRILL

Skill Development: Pitching (Swing length)
Levels: Beginner, Intermediate
Start Position: Setup in the usual manner for the pitch. Vary the length of the swing and observe the differences in feel and ball flight. The wrist break should happen naturally. Continue to swing with the arms and the shoulders with a firm target wrist. Use swing length of 3 to 3 and 4 to 4 for pitching. (Refer to figure 7-3.)
Evaluation: You have improved when you can relate the swing length to the distance required. If you cannot, revert to one target and one swing length.

TARGET DRILL

Skill Development: Pitching (Distance and direction)
Levels: Beginner, Intermediate, Advanced
Start Position: Setup as for the pitch using targets at thirty yards, forty yards, and fifty yards. Hit shots to each target. Use different clubs for the varied distances.
Evaluation: You are improving when you hit the targets consistently and you can adjust the swing length and choice of club for the appropriate distance. If you are missing the target on the right or left, revert to the clubs on the ground for the setup. If distance is the problem, revert to the swing length drill.

TARGET AND NONTARGET ARM DRILL

Skill Development: Pitching (Control)
Levels: Beginner, Intermediate, Advanced
Start Position: Setup as for a pitch with the club in the target or nontarget hand. Execute miniswings.
Evaluation: The results will become more consistent as you get stronger. You will also be able to make longer swings with practice.

TRACK DRILL

Skill Development: Pitching (Setup and swing)
Levels: Beginner, Intermediate, Advanced
Start Position: Use the golf clubs on the ground and setup parallel with a slightly open stance. The two clubs form a track, the clubhead moves back and through between the clubs.
Evaluation: You have improved when the swing path is natural and the clubhead does not touch the track. If you continue to hit the track during the swing, revert to elimination of the ball. Make swings using the track.

OVERLAP DRILL

Skill Development: Pitching (Control)
Levels: Beginner, Intermediate, Advanced
Start Position: Setup as for the pitch. Place rear hand over the target hand and swing. Do not incorporate a ball at the beginning. Make miniswings and increase to a 4 to 4 swing. Introduce the ball using the overlap drill as you begin to feel more control.
Evaluation: This will eliminate too much wrist break; it also necessitates control for the club. You are improving if you feel confident about introducing a ball. If this drill is too intimidating, revert to the target and nontarget arm drill for control.

Many of the drills for the full swing may be adapted for pitching.

PRACTICE

Introduce your practice of twenty-five repetitions, grip, align/aim, and setup. Here is an example of a practice program.

1. Toss balls into the air using the rear hand, in an underhanded stiff wrist action. Toss to different targets and different heights.
2. Pitch to various targets, various distances.
3. Pitch into an umbrella.
4. Use different clubs—9 iron, pitching wedge, sand wedge, or specialty wedges.
5. Vary swing length and grip up and down on the club.
6. Practice the different distances until you become familiar with club and swing length necessary for various distances.
7. Be competitive with yourself or a partner.

Performance Tip

Checklist for Pitching

1. Narrow, open stance
2. Grip down shaft
3. Weight on target side
4. Ball center to forward in stance
5. Swing 3 to 3 or 4 to 4
6. Slight wrist break
7. Small weight shift on 4 to 4 swing

SUMMARY

- The goal of the pitch shot is to stop the ball as close to the flag as possible. This requires a more lofted club than the club used for chipping. Clubs of choice are a 9 iron, pitching wedge, sand wedge, or lob wedge.
- A short pitch shot should be used when you are within twenty yards of the green or to get you over an obstacle between you and the flag.
- The long pitch shot has more air time and less roll and can be used by an advanced golfer from up to 100 yards out. This shot is an extension of the short pitch swing and a version of the full swing.
- Specialty pitching clubs are available with a greater degree of loft than the 9 iron, pitching wedge, or sand wedge.

CHAPTER 9

THE **FULL SWING:**
SKILLS

OBJECTIVES:

After reading this chapter, you should be able to do the following:

- Realize that the same tempo is required for all clubs.
- Understand why tempo, posture, and rhythm are a constant.
- Learn that setup and ball placement is crucial for good results.
- Understand the importance of hand position in the swing.
- Identify the principles of the full swing.
- Learn to adapt drills that will enhance the swing.

KEY TERMS

While reading this chapter, you will become familiar with the following terms:

▶ **Rhythm**
▶ **Target Line**
▶ **Tempo**

TEMPO

The full swing is swinging through the ball rather than hitting at the ball. The swing is a series of coordinated movements, turning and returning to the ball in sequence. The most important components of the full swing are **tempo, rhythm,** and the proper sequence of grip, stance, and posture. In chapter 5, using the twenty-five-repetition drill for grip, stance, alignment, and swing, we discussed the importance of becoming comfortable with the full swing before striking a ball. The full swing requires the same tempo for all the clubs from the driver to the pitching wedge. The only variations are in ball position and distance from the ball, which is dictated by the length of the club. Posture, tempo, and rhythm must remain constant throughout the swing. No one can tell you the ideal rhythm, but it may help to watch players with good rhythm. These players have a smooth, easy, and effortless swing. You must practice without a ball in order to build a simple repeatable swing, a swing that puts you in a position to repeatedly apply the club face squarely to the ball at impact. You have now developed a tempo that suits you, the swing is coordinated in proper sequence, and you have a feel for your swing.

SETUP

The setup for the full swing is the basic golf position and posture of the golfer at address. It includes the position of the feet on the ground shoulder width apart and the weight evenly distributed between the right and left sides. Bend or tilt from the hips, push the bottom out, keep the chin up, stand tall with a slight knee flex, and the arms hang naturally. The arms should be loose and the feet should feel light on the ground. The golfer will remain in this posture throughout the swing (see figure 9-1).

SWING

The arms swing and the body follows during the backswing. The hips lead, allowing arms, hands, rear shoulder, and the club head to arrive together during

---

▶ **Tempo**
 Developed through practice without a ball to build a simple repeatable swing that puts you in a position to apply the club face squarely to the ball at impact.

▶ **Rhythm**
 Essential in building up to the full swing, players with good rhythm have a smooth, easy, and effortless swing.

FIGURE 9-1 Setup for the full swing.

FIGURE 9-2 Turning away from the ball the arms swing and the body follows.

the downswing. You are turning away and returning to and through the ball (see figure 9-2). Turning and returning to the ball in sequence produces perfect timing.

BACKSWING OR TAKEAWAY

The shoulders and arms form a triangle at address. This must be maintained throughout the swing. The initial move in the takeaway is the movement of the target shoulder away from the target and behind the ball. The shoulder aims behind the chin. The club head should move away from the ball close to the ground for the first six to twelve inches. The target shoulder moves with the arms, hands, and club, therefore the club moves away inside the ball to **target line**. The target line is drawn through the ball straight to the target. The club is moved away maintaining the triangle and allowing a wide arc. The turn of the shoulders creates an upright swing; the club face on the takeaway remains square in relation to your body. The weight moves to the inside of the rear foot (the heel). The lower part of the body remains relatively still during the backswing. When your hands are in a position above your rear foot, the club should be parallel to the ground with the toe pointing to the sky. The rear elbow bends, and the club begins to move upwards. The rear elbow points down toward the ground and behind you (see figure 9-3).

FIGURE 9-3 At the height of the backswing the rear elbow points down.

FIGURE 9-4 To begin the downswing the arms drop down and turn.

TOP OF THE BACKSWING

At the top of the backswing the club is pointing down the ball to target line. The shaft is parallel to the ground. The target hand is square (flat) (see figure 9-10). The rear elbow remains pointing toward the ground. The target arm is across the chest. Hold onto the club with the last three fingers of the target hand; the thumb of the target hand is underneath the shaft (see figure 9-3).

DOWNSWING

The downswing is initiated with the lower body (see figure 9-4). The weight is transferred from the rear to the target side. Plant the target heel. The target hip clears or turns smoothly. The rear shoulder and the club head arrive at impact together. The impact position is similar to the position at setup except the weight is on the target side. Your head is behind the ball and the hips begin to turn toward

▶ **Target Line**
The target line is drawn through the ball straight to the target.

FIGURE 9-5 Impact position is similar to the position at setup except body weight is on the target side. The hips move through the target.

FIGURE 9-6 Impact.

the target. The arms drop down close to the rear hip and the body turns through (see figures 9-5 and 9-6).

FOLLOW-THROUGH

The body turns through the ball but the head remains in its impact position during the follow-through. The target elbow begins to bend and the rear arm extends. The rear forearm rotates over the target arm. The majority of the weight finishes on the target side, while a little weight remains on the toe of the rear leg. The rear knee is pointing toward the target. The hands and arms finish high over the target shoulder with the head, chest, and stomach facing the target. A balanced finish! The follow-through is a reflection of the backswing (see figures 9-7, 9-8, and 9-9).

IMPORTANCE OF HAND POSITION

The hands are the body's only connection to the club, therefore their position in relation to the body and swing path are important to the success of a shot. Be sure to check the hands at address (grip), position of the club and hands at hip level

FIGURE 9-7 Follow-through. The body turns through the ball and the head remains in its impact position.

FIGURE 9-8 The majority of the weight finishes on the target side with the rear knee pointing toward the target.

FIGURE 9-9 A balanced finish with the hands and arms high over the target shoulder. The head, chest, and stomach are facing the target.

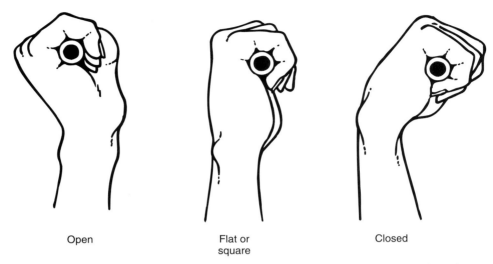

Open   Flat or   Closed
              square

FIGURE 9-10 The target hand should be square (flat), not open or closed.

(toe of club is pointing toward the sky), and the position of the hands at the top of the backswing (flat, square) (see figure 9-10).

IMPORTANCE OF PATH AND PLANE

To deliver the club squarely through the ball on the target line, the golfer must understand how the club should be swung through impact. Unless delivered from inside (that is, closer to the body) the imaginary line to the target, to square at impact, to the inside on the follow-through, a ball flight error will occur. From the top of the backswing, swing the club close to the body on the downswing and follow-through. The following guidelines help to promote an inside to straight to inside path of the downswing. (Refer to figure 10-2.)

- Weight at top of backswing, is on the inside of the rear foot. A good tip for weight transfer is to feel the weight over the rear knee and on the rear heel. This prevents too large a weight transfer.
- Knees flexed (slight flex in rear knee is necessary). A straight-locked rear (nontarget) knee is evident in a number of beginners.
- Plant the target heel. The lower body initiates downswing and arms and hands follow.
- Do not allow rear (nontarget) side to control the downswing. Target side leads, rear side follows.
- Swing from inside to square to inside.

Performance Tip

Principles of the Full Swing

- Check Grip
- Setup, align and aim
- Ball Placement
- Takeaway—Use the big muscle of the target shoulder
- Top of Backswing—Weight on the rear foot (inside heel)
- Downswing—Plant the target heel; target hip clears or turns smoothly, arms and hands follow
- Follow-through—Weight on the target side and belt buckle facing the target

DRILLS

As mentioned in chapter 6, practice drills can make for quality practice sessions. Specific areas of the swing should be practiced through the use of drills. One must already have the feel for the full swing. Using the teaching progression in this book, students will have developed a feel for the full swing. The swing may then be dissected to develop techniques and feel. Through the use of drills, movements may be isolated. There is no added pressure to remember the full swing. Drills are used for both positive reinforcement and the development of feel and proper technique in the swing. Adapt a drill beneficial to the problem area in the swing. For example, an error in the ball flight may necessitate a swing path drill. Have someone stand behind you looking down the line and then facing you to determine the necessary drill for correction.

GRIP DRILL

▶ Full Swing Grip

Skill Development: Full Swing (Grip)
Levels: Beginner, Intermediate, Advanced
Start Position: Take the club in the rear hand with the appropriate grip. The Vs formed by the thumb and index finger of both hands should point between the

chin and rear shoulder. Grip the club with a strong grip. The rear hand is too far under the shaft and the target hand is moved over to the rear side (four knuckles showing). Adapt a weak grip. The target hand is turned too far towards the target (no knuckles showing). The rear hand also moved towards the target.

Evaluation: You are improving once you can differentiate between a neutral, strong, and weak grip. Continue to grip and regrip until the neutral grip becomes natural.

SETUP DRILL

▶ Setup/Free Swings

Skill Development: Full Swing
Level: Beginners
Start Position: Move into the setup position; do not incorporate a club or ball. Practice swinging with the arms hanging naturally. You should feel relaxed.
Evaluation: You have improved once you can adapt this position in a relaxed manner with relaxed shoulders, arms, and legs.
Skill Development: Full Swing (Setup)
Levels: Beginners, Intermediate, Advanced
Start Position: Use clubs on the ground and setup parallel (railway tracks). Setup parallel to the clubs aiming at a target.
Evaluation: You have improved once you can take this setup without the aid of a track on the ground. Introduce a ball, and hit some shots to the target. You have improved if you hit the target. If you do not hit the target, revert to hitting balls using the tracks. If the balls hit while using the track were not on target, you may need to adapt a Swing Path Drill. Setup is probably not the problem.
Skill Development: Full Swing (Setup)
Levels: Beginners, Intermediate
Start Position: Use clubs or boards on ground for a square, open, and closed stance (see figure 9-11). Setup parallel to the boards in a square position. Adjust the position for an open stance and a closed stance.
Evaluation: You have improved when you can adapt all three positions without the boards. If you do not feel comfortable or confident, ask a partner to check each position.

PATH DRILL

▶ Board Drill

Skill Development: Swing (Path)
Levels: Beginner, Intermediate, Advanced

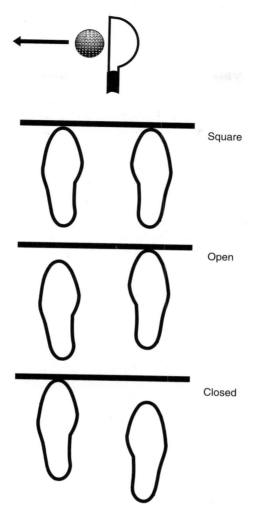

FIGURE 9-11 Square, open, and closed starting positions for full swing setup drill.

Start Position: Use a board flat on the ground beside the ball (on the right side for the right-handed golfer, (reverse for the left-handed golfer). If the board interferes with the backswing or the down swing, the club path is incorrect. Always make sure that the board extends one to two feet behind the ball position so that you will never hit the end of board.

Evaluation: Once you have practiced the swing without the use of a ball and succeeded in avoiding the board, introduce a ball. You have improved if you continue to hit balls and never contact the board. You need to revert to the tee drill if you are nervous with the Board Drill or you continuously strike the board. You could also use a club box on the ground. If you hit the box, it will not hurt you or your club.

▶ **Tee Drill**

Skill Development: Swing (Path)
Levels: Beginner, Intermediate
Start Position: Place one tee twelve inches in front and one tee twelve inches behind the ball. Use the tees to guide the backswing and follow-through.
Evaluation: You have improved when the ball flight is consistently on target. If an error in ball flight continues, use miniswings until you feel comfortable with the in to in swing path.

WEIGHT TRANSFER DRILL

▶ **Baseball Drill**

Skill Development: Full Swing (Weight transfer)
Levels: Beginner, Intermediate
Start Position: Setup as for full swing. Slide the target foot over to the rear foot. Make the backswing and hold the position at the top for a split second. Return the target foot to the original position and execute the downswing and the follow-through. Coordination will take time so be patient! Also use this drill for timing. Practice without the ball initially.
Evaluation: You have improved if you can feel a difference in the ease of the swing even without hitting a ball. Introduce a ball and continue the drill. If the weight transfer feels more comfortable and the ball flight more consistent, you have improved. If the results are not positive, revert to the drill without the ball.

▶ **Buckle Drill**

Skill Development: Full Swing (Weight transfer)
Level: Beginner
Start Position: Make swings with and without the club. Turn your back to the target on the backswing and turn your belt buckle to the target on the follow-through. Transfer the weight back and through. Be aware of coil and uncoil. Turn and return to the ball.
Evaluation: You should feel that your arms are swinging naturally and the weight transfer happens with little effort. Use the audio key to suit your tempo; for example, back to target, belt to target, or turn and return. When you introduce the club you should feel a relaxed swing and easy weight transfer. Remember, weight transfer does not call for a big physical movement; the weight only goes to the inside of the rear foot.

▶ Go For It Drill

Skill Development: Full Swing (Weight transfer)
Levels: Intermediate, Advanced
Start Position: Put eight to ten balls in a line a few inches apart. Stand away from ball number one and make a few full swings. Move toward the line of balls; hit the first ball and continue to swing and hit each ball. Keep a smooth, fluid swing. As you move forward, your weight is on the rear foot. Step forward with your target foot and the forward swing begins. Step forward with the rear foot and the backswing begins. Be patient! Coordination is difficult, but once mastered the student will develop wonderful feel and balance. Practice without the balls initially.
Evaluation: Once you have mastered this drill without the ball, you have begun to understand weight transfer. Introduce the balls; ball flight should be more consistent and the whole swing should be effortless. If weight transfer remains a physical movement, you must return to this drill without the use of balls.

▶ Knee Drill

Skill Development: Full Swing (Weight transfer)
Level: Beginner
Start Position: Swing with or without a club. Move the target knee to the rear knee and the rear knee to the target knee. On the backswing bring the target knee to the rear knee. On the downswing bring the rear knee to the target knee.
Evaluation: Use a mirror for visual feedback. If the lower body is too active, too much movement to the rear side on the backswing, have another person put his or her hand on your rear hip on the backswing. If there is a lateral movement, the person will feel it when holding the rear hip. The person assisting should kneel down behind you as if in the setup position; this eliminates the possibility of injury. Use the mirror again to check for improvement.

▶ Upslope Drill

Skill Development: Full Swing (Weight transfer)
Levels: Beginner, Intermediate, Advanced
Start Position: Hit balls from an uphill lie. This creates the feel of getting behind the ball and back to the rear side.
Evaluation: Return to hitting balls from a flat lie. The weight transfer should feel effortless. If you notice no improvement return to the upslope and swing without the ball.

▶ **Weight Drill**

Skill Development: Full Swing (Weight transfer)
Level: Beginner
Start Position: Move weight to the rear foot and move weight to the target foot. Repeat. The golfer takes the usual setup and makes swings repeating the phrase, "Weight back and weight through." Practice with and without the club. On the backswing the weight transfers to the rear foot and on the downswing weight transfers to the target foot.
Evaluation: Visual feedback is an excellent way to learn. The back and through move should occur without a huge physical effort. If this occurs you are beginning to understand weight transfer.

▶ **2″ × 4″ Weight Transfer Drill**

Skill Development: Full Swing (Weight transfer)
Levels: Beginner, Intermediate
Start Position: Place a 2″ × 4″ board under the outside edge of the rear foot. You may substitute an old shaft with the grip end under the outside of the foot. Swing and you will notice it is no longer possible to let the weight go to the outside of the rear foot.
Evaluation: Without the use of the board or old shaft, make swings and feel the difference. If you notice that there is not a huge weight transfer you are improving. Hit balls; if the weight finishes consistently on the target foot and the ball on target, you have improved. If no improvement occurs revert to the Baseball Drill.

TARGET AWARENESS DRILL

▶ **Cane Drill**

Skill Development: Full Swing (Firm target side)
Level: Beginner
Start Position: Setup as for the swing. Invert a club in the rear hand and place it on the ground as a cane. Swing the target arm back and through. Pull with target side to finish. This eliminates too big a backswing and places emphasis on the follow-through. The energy is used in the follow-through.
Evaluation: Feel a firmness on the target side through impact. When this occurs you are becoming more aware of the proper feeling on the target side. Make normal swings with the club emphasizing firmness through impact and on the follow-through. If this feeling is not acquired, adapt the Towel Drill.

▶ Nontarget Hand Off at Impact

Skill Development: Full Swing (Firm target side)
Levels: Intermediate, Advanced
Start Position: Setup as for the normal swing. Swing the club but release the rear hand after impact. If you do not have enough strength and control do not attempt this drill.
Evaluation: If ball flight is straight, improvement has occurred. This drill will not be successful if the rear side is too aggressive or if the target side is too weak. If you are unable to master this drill, try it without the ball, then reintroduce the ball.

▶ Nontarget Hand Off

Skill Development: Full Swing (Firm target side)
Levels: Intermediate, Advanced
Start Position: Swing with the club in the target hand only. Hit some balls using target hand only.
Evaluation: You are improving if you can master this without the ball. Introduce the ball; if you can hit the ball toward the target you have improved. If hitting the ball is difficult, revert to the drill without the ball. As the target side becomes stronger, your success rate will improve.

▶ Overlap Drill

Skill Development: Full Swing (Target side awareness, Position at the top of the backswing, angle of attack)
Levels: Beginner, Intermediate, Advanced
Start Position: Grip the club with the target hand; place the rear hand completely over the target hand and swing. The target hand at the top of the backswing will be unable to open or close. This is also an excellent drill for the golfer who tries to strike the ball with the rear hand.
Evaluation: Improvement has occurred when you can hit balls effortlessly with this drill. If you overswing you will not be able to hit the ball crisply. You will remain firm through impact as the rear side is unable to dominate. If no improvement occurs, practice without the ball until the feeling is achieved.

▶ Towel Drill

Skill Development: Full Swing (Firm target side)
Level: Beginner
Start Position: Use a towel in the target hand and make full swings.
Evaluation: You have improved when you can relate to a firm target side through impact. If this drill does not create this feeling adapt the whoosher drill.

▶ Whoosher Drill

Skill Development: Full Swing (Firm target side)
Levels: Beginner, Intermediate, Advanced
Start Position: Use the wooden clubs; invert the club and hold the club just above the head of the club in the target hand. Rear hand is on the rear hip. Swing the club back and through. Where do you hear the "whoosh"? You should hear the whoosh sound just at impact. Rear hand on the hip will promote the lower body motion.
Evaluation: If you achieve the whoosh at impact you have improved. Swing normally feeling that same acceleration through the ball. If this does not occur practice the Towel Drill to promote the feeling.

TEMPO DRILL

▶ Feet Together Drill

Skill Development: Full Swing (Tempo)
Levels: Beginner, Intermediate, Advanced
Start Position: Set up with both feet together. Using the club, make full swings. This drill will slow down the swing. If you swing too fast you will lose balance.
Evaluation: When you finish in balance you are improving. Hit balls using the same drill. You are improving if you hit the ball on target and finish in balance. If you do not notice improvement, practice the drill again without the ball.

▶ Go For It Drill

Skill Development: Full Swing (Tempo)
Levels: Intermediate, Advanced
Start Position: See "Go For It Drill" (Weight transfer) discussed previously
Evaluation: If you are hitting every ball without breaking the rhythm of the drill you have improved. If the results are inconsistent return to the drill without the balls or swing with the feet together.

▶ Toe Drill

Skill Development: Full Swing (Tempo)
Levels: Beginner, Intermediate, Advanced
Start Position: The target foot is on the ground and the rear foot has just the toes balancing on the ground. Make swings. If you create too much lower body movement you will lose balance. Use this to get the feeling of your arms and hands in the swing.
Evaluation: You have improved if you finish in balance. If you lose balance, you are swinging too hard. Return to the Feet Together Drill to improve tempo.

RELEASE DRILL

▶ **Split Hands Drill**

Skill Development: Full Swing (Release)
Levels: Beginners, Intermediate, Advanced
Start Position: Move the rear hand down the shaft grip with the target hand at the top. Leave a gap of about four inches between hands. This helps the rear arm rotate over the target arm. It helps to promote a forward swing path that comes from the inside. It also creates the feel of swinging down through the ball.
Evaluation: If there is an improvement in feel without the ball, hit some balls using the drill. When the results are on target, take your normal grip and hit balls. The feeling should be noticeably different and the results on target. If no difference is observed, return to the drill without the ball.

EXTRA DRILLS

▶ **Head Control Drill**

Skill Development: Full Swing (Steady head)
Levels: Beginner, Intermediate, Advanced
Start Position: Use a partner or the wall. This drill determines excessive lateral movement of the head. The partner faces the student and reaches the arm out to hold the student's head; student swings without the club for safety reasons. The student may also set up to the wall with top of the head against the wall. Use a cushion between the head and the wall.
Evaluation: Use feedback from the partner. If the head continues to move, decrease the backswing. You have improved when you can swing freely without head movement.

▶ **Hit and Hold Drill**

Skill Development: Full Swing (Acceleration through to the target)
Levels: Beginner, Intermediate, Advanced
Start Position: Make your usual swing but hold the follow-through at waist height. This makes you swing through and down the line; it stops you from making a wristy movement. It requires acceleration through the ball.
Evaluation: You have improved when you can hold that finish position at waist height. If you are unable to finish low, place a tee twelve inches in front of the ball and swing over it.

▶ **Target Drill**

Skill Development: Full Swing (Distance)
Levels: Beginner, Intermediate, Advanced
Start Position: Hit balls to the different targets. Use objects in the ground at regular intervals. Swing out to the target.
Evaluation: You have improved when you can relate club selection to distance.

> **Drills can be fun. Set a high standard and be prepared to reach it!**

PRACTICE

Introduce your practice of twenty-five repetitions for grip, align/aim, and setup. Here is an example of a practice program.
1. Place clubs on the ground for alignment.
2. Hit balls, concentrating on the follow-through.
3. Introduce a target side awareness drill, rear hand off the club at impact.
4. Introduce a tempo drill; swing with both feet together.
5. Use targets.
6. Use Setup routine for every shot.
7. Make practice time quality time.

To lower your scores practice the game the way it is scored, about 63 percent short game and 37 percent long game.

Performance Tip

Checklist for the Full Swing

1. Check Grip
2. Setup, Align and Aim
3. Ball Placement
4. Takeaway: Use the big muscle of the target shoulder
5. Top of Backswing: Place the weight on the rear foot (inside heel)
6. Downswing: Clear target hip, plant the target heel. The arms and the hands should follow.
7. Follow-through: Weight on the target side and belt buckle facing the target

SUMMARY

- The most important components of the full swing are tempo, rhythm, and the proper sequence of grip, stance, and posture.
- The full swing requires the same tempo for all clubs, driver through pitching wedge, and only requires simple variations in position and distance from the ball depending on the length of the club being used.
- The hands are the body's only connection to the club, therefore their position in relation to the body and swing path are important to the success of a shot. Correct hand placement at address and a square or flat position at the top of the back swing is essential.
- An inside to straight to inside path of the downswing will decrease the chance of ball flight error.

Assessment 9-1

Full Swing Evaluation

Name _____ Section _____ Date _____

Testing with the aid of a swing analysis. If you have followed the learning style, you will feel most comfortable with this method. There is no need for a ball. Use the analysis sheet to evaluate yourself; check off each area as you improve. You must use the expertise of the teacher, who will check each area and award points from 0 to 5; a score of 5 is excellent for each area.

SWING ANALYSIS

Student takes practice swings without a ball. Teacher observes certain checkpoints.

Comments

a. Looking down target line
   from behind the ball.   _____

b. Club in right hand (reverse
   for left-handed golfer).   _____

c. Grip.   _____

d. Setup/square club face.   _____

e. Takeaway.   _____

f. Position of left hand at top
   of backswing (reverse for
   left-handed golfer).   _____

g. Weight transfer.   _____

h. Downswing.   _____

i. Impact.   _____

j. Follow-through.   _____

k. Hold the finish.   _____

The instructor may write their own swing analysis sheet or use a different grading system, but always leave room for positive comments (see table 9-1). The student must see the results and have some positive reinforcement. The student needs to go away with constructive criticism and have new goals.

Work on your weaknesses. Continue to practice your strengths. Have you improved? The swing analysis may have all of these checkpoints or may be more concise. This is the teacher's choice.

TABLE 9-1
Swing Checklist

Points Possible = 55	5 Points for Each Concept	Rating	Comment
Check	**Concept**		
Picking Spot	Go behind the ball/club in the right hand		
Address and Grip	Hands on the club		
Stance	Relaxed, feet are shoulder width apart		
Posture	Chin up, bottom out, flexed from hips, slight knee bend, and arms hang naturally		
Clubhead	Face square		
Takeaway	Thigh, arms, and club move as a unit for complete shoulder turn. Weight is transferred to nontarget foot		
Top of Backswing	Position of left hand and extension of arm (vice versa for a left-handed golfer)		
Downswing	Activate with the lower body, arms and club to follow. Maintain the angle of hands and club		
Impact	Firm target side, head steady through impact. Arm rotation nontarget over target		
Finish	Face the target, weight on the target side. Teacher should see sole on nontarget shoe		
Overall Swing	Balanced		
	Total		

CHAPTER 10

UNDERSTANDING BALL FLIGHT:
COMMON PROBLEMS

UNDERSTANDING

OBJECTIVES

After reading this chapter, you should be able to do the following:

- Understand the factors that influence a ball's flight.
- Identify how ball flight is influenced by club face and club path.
- Isolate problems with ball flight and make corrections.
- Recognize the most common problems for beginners.

KEY TERMS

While reading this chapter, you will become familiar with the following terms:

► **Club Face Position**
► **Club Path**

WHY A BALL FLIES THE WAY IT DOES

All golfers should be able to make corrections to their swing by understanding why a ball flies the way it does. You will learn to read the feedback from the balls you hit by understanding how swing path or club face position causes a ball to hit the target or fly right or left of your intended target.

BALL FLIGHT

There are nine possible flight directions (see figure 10-1), and these directions are influenced by two primary laws (discussed in chapter 5)—**club path** and **club face position.**

The three possible club paths are in to in, in to out, and out to in.

The initial direction of the ball is determined by these swing paths. The ball starts out on target with the in to in club path (see figure 10-2). With the in to out club path (see figure 10-3), the result for the right-handed golfer is the ball begins right of target and for the left-handed golfer the ball begins left of target. The out to in club path result (see figure 10-4) for the right-handed golfer is the ball begins left of the target and for the left-handed golfer the ball begins right of the target.

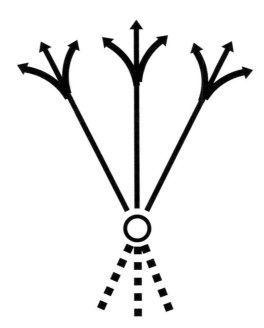

FIGURE 10-1 Once a ball is hit there are nine possible flight directions.

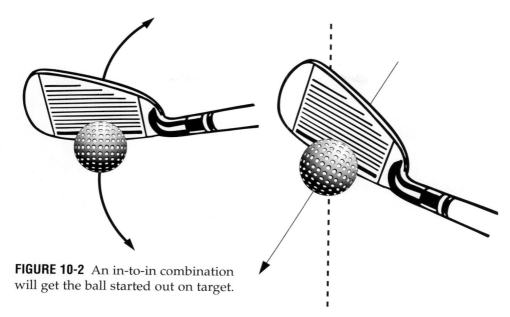

FIGURE 10-2 An in-to-in combination will get the ball started out on target.

FIGURE 10-3 An in-to-out swing path by a right-handed golfer results in a push that gets the ball started right of the target (left of the target for left-handed golfers).

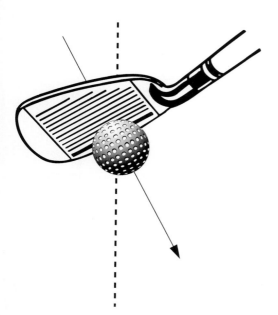

FIGURE 10-4 An out-to-in swing path creates a pull that starts the ball out left of the target in right-handed golfers and right of the target in left-handed golfers.

▶ **Club Path**

The initial direction of the ball is determined by an in-to-in, in-to-out or out-to-in club (swing) path. An in-to-in swing path will get the ball started on target while an in-to-out or an out-to-in path will result in an initial push or pull of the ball.

▶ **Club Face Position**

A square, open or closed club face position is responsible for any final curvature of a ball in flight relative to its swing path.

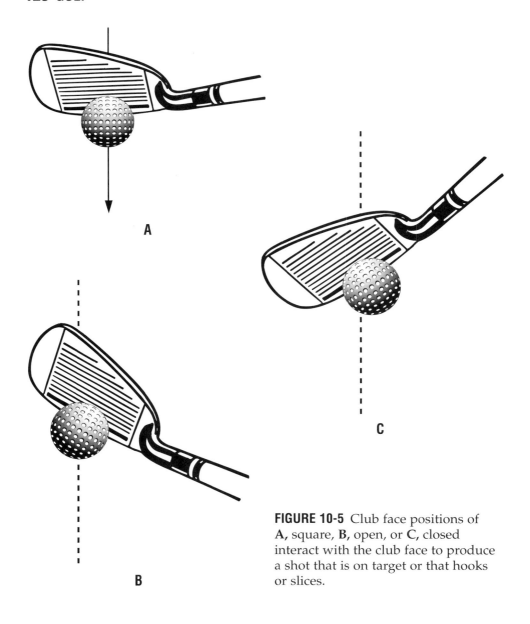

A

C

B

FIGURE 10-5 Club face positions of **A,** square, **B,** open, or **C,** closed interact with the club face to produce a shot that is on target or that hooks or slices.

The results of these three swing paths are on target, right of target, or left of target (reverse for the left-handed golfer). Any final curvature of the balls flight results from the club face position relative to these paths. The three club face positions are square, open, and closed (see figure 10-5a, b, and c).

A combination of the club face and the club path determines the initial direction and curvature of the ball. The toe striking the ball first has a tendency to pro-

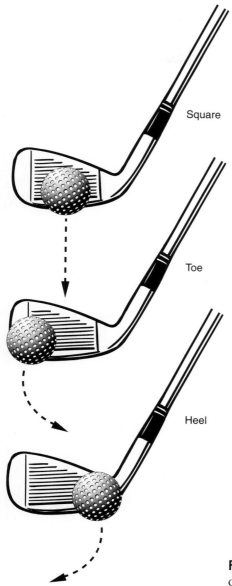

Square

Toe

Heel

FIGURE 10-6 Club face position and affects on ball flight.

duce a hook. The heel striking the ball first has a tendency to produce a slice (see figure 10-6). A swing path of in to out combined with a closed club face will cause the ball to travel from right to left and finish far left of the target. This is a hook (reverse for the left-handed golfer). A swing path of out to in combined with an open club face will cause the ball to travel from left to right and finish far right of the target. This is a slice (reverse for the left-handed golfer).

Understanding why the ball flies in different curvatures should help you identify problems and make corrections. Studying table 10–1 should give you a few clues on how to improve your accuracy.

The most common problems of incorrect club path are push, pull, hook, and slice. Beginners may also experience one or all of the problems listed in table 10-2 in the early stages of their game.

An understanding of club path and club face position will help you diagnose the fault. If problems persist, seek the help of your professional. The longer you try to use a quick fix, the longer you will take to eliminate the problem. Your professional can usually diagnose and correct the problem immediately.

TABLE 10-1
Problems, Causes, and Corrections to Ball Flight

	Problem	Cause	Correction
Grip	Hook	Hands too strong, see too many knuckles on target hand	Regrip: Move hands towards the target
Grip	Slice	Hands too weak	Regrip: Move hands away from target
Setup	Hook	Stance: Feet closed and grip strong	Regrip and square stance
Setup	Slice	Stance: Feet open and grip weak	Regrip and square stance
Setup	Hook	Close club face	Square club face
Setup	Slice	Open club face	Square club face
Takeaway	Incorrect path	Taking club back too far on the outside or inside	Place a tee 12″ behind ball and take the club over the tee
Takeaway	Slice or pull	Pick the club straight up with the hands	Remain in the triangle formed by the club and the arms
Takeaway	Inconsistent results	Excessive lower body movement	Steady the lower body
Takeaway	The ball goes right of target (reverse for left-handed golfer)	Reverse pivot: The weight is on the target side before the hands get to the top of the backswing.	Practice Baseball Weight Transfer Drill
Takeaway	Pull	Taking the club away from the ball with arms only	Concentrate on the target shoulder, club and arms moving together
Takeaway	Inconsistent results	Head sways	Practice Head Drill and Wall Drill
Takeaway	Inconsistent results	Weak right or left side; right or left side collapses	Practice Target Side Awareness Drill; firm up at impact
Top of Backswing	Slice or pull	Letting go of the club at the top	Hold on to the club with the last three fingers of the target hand
Downswing	Slice, pull, hitting heavy, no distance	Throwing the club at the ball, "casting"	Keep the angle between the club and the arms on the downswing

TABLE 10-1
Continued

	Problem	Cause	Correction
Downswing	Whiff (complete miss)	Straightening up out of posture	Keep knees soft at address. The rear knee slightly flexed when you arrive at the top of the backswing, remain in posture throughout the swing
Downswing	Whiff	Bent target arm	Take the elbow away with emphasis on the target shoulder; this should eliminate bent elbow
Impact	Pull or lack of power	Collapse at impact	Practice Whooser Drill and Hit and Hold Drill
Impact	Ball right of target (reverse for left-handed golfer)	Getting ahead of the ball	Hold the Head Drill; concentrate on watching the back of the ball through impact
Follow-through	Slice	No extension through the ball	Swing out towards the target. Practice the Hit and Hold Drill

TABLE 10-2
Problems Often Faced by Beginners

Problem—Topping	
Causes	**Corrections**
Out-to-in swing path	Use Board Drill for swing path
Not remaining in posture throughout the swing; lifting upper body and straightening the legs	Posture should remain constant throughout the swing; use a mirror for feedback
Leaving the weight on the rear side	Transfer the weight: Weight Transfer Drill
Arm swinging or the rear arm leading the downswing	Use the large muscles of the lower body to initiate the downswing
Helping the club head get the ball airborne	Keep the hands ahead of the clubhead
Ball too far forward in the stance	Position the ball in the center of the stance
Collapsing the target side	Keep the target side firm through impact
The rear arm leading the downswing	Setup with the feet together and initiate a smooth swing; rear side remains passive: Overlap Drill

Continued

TABLE 10-2
Continued

Problem—Hitting Behind the Ball	
Causes	**Corrections**
Picking the club up on the takeaway	Take the club away from the ball along the ground: Tee Drill
Casting the club with the hands on the downswing	Keep the angle between the arms and the club on the downswing
Dropping the rear shoulder on the downswing	Turn the shoulders back level through the ball
Having the weight on the target side at the top of the backswing	Practice Weight Transfer Drill
Problem—Shanking	
Causes	**Corrections**
The ball catches the hosel of the club	Allow the target hand to remain facing the target on the takeaway
A hurried backswing	Take the club away slowly on the target line rather than inside
Getting ahead of the ball at impact	Do not slide the hips ahead of the ball on the downswing
Too much weight on the toes at address	Move weight toward the balls of the feet
The grip is too tight	Loosen the grip
The shoulders and the hips open too quickly on the downswing	The impact position is similar to the setup except the weight has transferred to the target side
A severe in-to-out swing path	Use Path Drill
Swinging the arms away from the body	Swing towards the rear hip on the downswing allowing the arms to remain close to the chest

SUMMARY

- Putting to use your knowledge of the combined affect of club path and club face on ball flight will allow you to diagnose problems with ball flight and make corrections.
- Problems with grip, setup, take away, top of backswing, downswing, impact, and follow-through have noticeable and predictable results on ball flight—all can be corrected with practice!
- Drills introduced earlier in the book can be used to help compensate for problems with topping, hitting behind the ball, and shanking.

CHAPTER 11

HITTING **SAND SHOTS:**
SKILLS

OBJECTIVES

After reading this chapter, you should be able to do the following:

- Understand that with practice sand play can be the least difficult shot.
- Learn proper execution for the most common sand shots.
- Detail the principles of sound sand play.
- Be able to improve sand play by incorporating drills.

KEY TERMS

While reading this chapter, you will become familiar with the following terms:

► **Ground the Club**
► **Hazard**

CONFIDENCE

Possibly the least difficult shot in golf is the bunker shot, and it is the one most feared. Most golfers do not get the opportunity to practice this shot and may not even find themselves in the sand bunker during a round of golf. When they eventually land in a bunker they are intimidated by the sand and do not feel comfortable with the adjustments necessary to play the shot successfully. From the bunker, the golfer may have to play long shots from fairway bunkers or shorter shots from around the green. These bunkers have been placed with plenty of thought to catch stray drives from the tee or errant approach shots to the green. With proper technique and one or two hours of practice you will be able to approach these shots with confidence, the same way you tackle a chip or pitch from the fairway. Eliminating fear in the bunker comes with sound fundamentals and practice. Approach bunkers with full confidence in yourself and with the goal of getting out of the sand.

HAZARD

A sand bunker is considered a **hazard.** The bunker is full of sand and a golfer is not allowed to **ground the club** in the sand before the stroke. The sole of the club may not touch (lie on) the sand when addressing the ball or during the backswing (you may take a practice swing while in the bunker, but you must not touch the sand with the club). Grounding the club in the sand incurs a two-stroke penalty. Different bunker situations will require adjustments in technique but all will have one thing in common: the sand. Before playing any bunker shot, you must observe the lie in the bunker, the type of sand (dry and fluffy or hard and wet), the lip on the bunker, and the distance from the flag.

SHOTS

The most common shots are: explosion, buried lie, uphill lie, downhill lie, and fairway.

▶ **Hazard**
Term used for bunkers and water hazards on the course.

▶ **Ground the club**
The sole of the club may not touch (lie on) the sand when addressing the ball or during the backswing. Grounding the club in the sand incurs a two-stroke penalty.

FIGURE 11-1 Drawing an imaginary dollar bill in the sand around the ball and then using the sand wedge to toss a dollar's worth of sand onto the green will help you execute a good bunker shot.

EXPLOSION SHOT

Play the explosion shot with a sand wedge. Survey the texture of the sand and the position of the ball in the sand, and whether or not there is a high lip (front) to the bunker. When playing the stroke from the sand think in terms of removing a rectangular piece of sand from the bunker. Think of tossing this sand onto the green. Draw an imaginary dollar bill in the sand around the ball. Using the sand wedge, toss a dollar's worth of sand onto the green (see figure 11-1). Dig or shuffle your feet into the sand to gain a firm stance and obtain feedback as to the type of sand. Grip down the shaft. Before you take your grip be sure to open the club face. Take the club in your rear hand and open the face; grip with the target hand and adjust to the appropriate grip with the rear hand. Take a slightly weaker grip than normal, moving the target hand more toward the target. You will swing more upright on the backswing with a restricted pivot. Open your stance, aim left of target for right-handed golfers (reverse for left-handed golfers). Place the ball forward of center toward the target foot with weight on the target side and the eyes on a spot two inches behind the ball. Make a three-fourths swing, swing through the sand on the spot two inches behind the ball, and follow-through. Make a swing that is slow and smooth. Finish with the weight on the target side. The club face never turns over through impact. By striking two inches behind the ball the sand pops the ball up and the club face never touches the ball. Swing the club through the back of the imaginary dollar bill and out the front, popping the ball onto the green. You must not touch the ball; if you hit the ball clean it will fly too far. Always think of the sand first. Focus on the sand behind the ball, not the ball.

▶ Adjustments

Playing from very fine sand requires you to take a shallow amount of sand. From coarser sand take a deeper amount and from wet sand take the least amount. Always focus on the two inches behind the ball. When a shallow divot of sand is required, take less of an upright backswing. For longer distances, take a longer follow-through and speed up the tempo of the swing. For the shorter shots, have a slower tempo and shorter follow-through. A putter may be used from the greenside bunker if there is no lip (a high front). Place the ball back in the stance and make a putting stroke. Remember you will have to swing a little harder than on the putting green to clear the sand and the intermediate terrain.

BURIED LIE

A buried lie can be very intimidating because the ball is covered with sand and you can barely see the top of the ball. The following adjustments must be made in the stance, the face of the club, and the swing. Take your grip as for the full swing and then close the face. Have a square stance and place the ball in the center of the stance. Distribute your weight equally. Make a shorter backswing and hit into the sand about two inches behind the ball and finish at the ball. Keep the target wrist firm in the follow-through. There is a short follow-through. Keep your hands ahead of the club head. Remember this ball will come out of the bunker on a low trajectory and will roll more than the explosion shot.

UPHILL BUNKER SHOT

Remember when playing from an upslope the ball will have a higher trajectory and therefore will travel a shorter distance. Play with an open stance and a square

Performance Tip

Principles of Sand Play

1. Dig the feet into the sand (may need to grip down the shaft as the hands become closer to the ground).
2. Open stance: Place the ball towards the target side (see figure below).
3. Upright swing: Keep the lower body quiet on the backswing, make a shoulder turn.
4. Downswing: Shift weight and follow through. Swing through a spot two inches behind the ball. The club face never turns over through impact.
5. Swing should be slow and smooth.

When hitting from the bunker keep an open stance with the ball toward the target side.

club face. Do not lean into the hill or the club face will dig into the sand. Body weight should be kept on the rear foot. Hit the sand slightly closer to the ball than for the normal shot. Make a fuller swing and keep the shoulders level with the slope. Make a smooth swing.

DOWNHILL BUNKER SHOT

The downhill bunker shot is possibly the most difficult of all the bunkers shots. The back lip of the bunker restricts the backswing. Using a normal grip, setup in an open stance, with your weight on the forward side. Place the ball in the back of the stance. Make an upright swing and keep the shoulders parallel with the contour of the ground. Hit about one inch behind the ball. Follow-through and the ball will roll on landing.

FAIRWAY BUNKER SHOT

The fairway bunker shot may be played like an ordinary shot. Distribute your weight evenly or even on the rear side for balance. Grip down on the shaft, and place your hands ahead of the ball. Your head remains steady. The main objective is to pick the ball clean from the sand. Try to keep your rear heel on the sand until after impact. The club to use is very dependent on the lie and the lip. You may use irons or woods from the fairway bunker depending on the lie. For beginners a 5 or 6 iron is recommended. If the ball lies close to the front lip of the bunker and the lip is high, a more lofted club will be necessary.

The club recommended for bunker shots around the green is the sand wedge (see figure 11-2). You should practice with this club and learn to play an explosion shot with confidence.

Performance Tip

Checklist for Successful Sand Shots

1. The first priority is to get the ball out of the sand.
2. Grip down the shaft with a weak grip.
3. Dig your feet into the sand.
4. Open your stance.
5. Focus on a line two inches behind the ball; swing through the dollar bill.
6. Swing through the ball with a slow, smooth tempo.

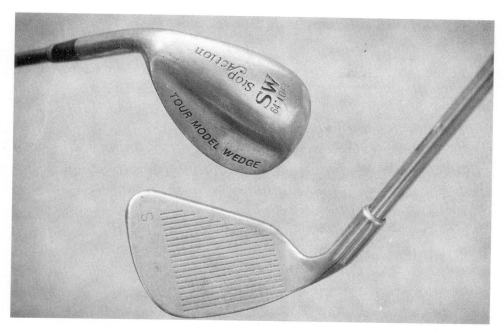

FIGURE 11-2 Sand wedge.

DRILLS

DOLLAR BILL DRILL

Skill Development: Sand Shot
Levels: Beginner, Intermediate
Start Position: Draw rectangular shapes in the sand and make practice swings through the shapes. Imagine that the ball is in the center, and set the leading edge of the club to the back line; this is where the club should enter the sand.
Evaluation: You have improved when you can swing through the back and the front of the imaginary dollar bill. Introduce a ball. If you continue to leave the ball in the sand, return to the drill. You have improved when you feel confident about getting every ball out of the sand.

TEMPO DRILLS

Skill Development: Sand Play (Tempo)
Levels: Beginner, Intermediate, Advanced
Start Position: Make swings with your eyes closed. Tempo is most important for bunker play. A slow swing is essential.

Evaluation: If you consistently remove the ball from the sand, you have improved. If the swing is still hurried, return to the Tempo Drill.

OVERWRAP DRILL

Skill Development: Sand Play (Tempo)
Levels: Beginner, Intermediate, Advanced
Start Position: Place the target hand on the club and the rear hand directly over it. Make swings.
Evaluation: Grip as for a sand shot. If you continue to remove the ball from the sand, the tempo has improved. If the ball remains in the sand, practice the drill again.

ALTERNATE TARGET DRILL

Skill Development: Sand Play (Distance)
Levels: Beginner, Intermediate, Advanced
Start Position: Play a short shot and a long shot.
Evaluation: If you reach the target consistently, you have improved. If you are inconsistent, practice taking a lot of sand and a small amount of sand. Make a shorter and a longer follow-through. Note the difference in each situation. Adapt the drills for the pitch shot for bunker play.

PRACTICE

Introduce your practice of twenty-five repetitions: grip, align/aim, and setup. Here is a practice program.

1. Make six dollar bill shapes in the sand and practice swinging through the dollar bill (no ball).
2. Continue with the dollar bill and place the ball in the center. Play explosion shots.
3. Do the same practice without the markings on the sand.
4. Practice buried lie shots.
5. Practice to different targets.
6. Alternate long and short shots.
7. Practice fairway shots from different positions in the bunker.
8. Practice until confident.
9. Learn to rake the bunker.
10. Remember you may only remove humanmade objects from the bunker before your stroke. A box or candy paper may be removed but a twig or leaf may not be removed.
11. Practice shots from grassy areas within the bunker; if the ball lands on grass within the bunker, you may ground the club without penalty.

Performance Tip

Practice Checklist

1. Practice in sand.
2. Swing must be slow and smooth.
3. Swing through the sand—those with fear of sand will stop the swing and leave the ball in the sand.
4. Concentrate on a spot two inches behind the ball in the sand.
5. For a shorter, higher shot, open the club face. For a longer shot, square the club face.

SUMMARY

- Practicing the fundamentals is the key to developing the confidence you will need to hit all types of bunker shots.
- Grounding the club in the sand before hitting a bunker shot incurs a two-stroke penalty.
- The target area for the explosion, buried lie, uphill lie, downhill lie, and fairway bunker shots should be a space one to two inches behind the ball so that the sand, not the club, pops the ball free.

UNDERSTANDING **UNEVEN LIES:**
STRATEGY

OBJECTIVES

After reading this chapter, you should be able to do the following:

- Explain why it is important to practice shots from uneven lies.
- Understand the adjustments necessary for uphill, downhill, and sidehill lies.
- Learn to draw and fade.
- Use the punch shot for recovery.
- Understand how wind can affect ball flight.
- Use drills to improve your swing on a hilly lie.

KEY TERMS

While reading this chapter, you will become familiar with the following terms:

► **Draw**
► **Fade**
► **Punch Shot**

FIGURE 12-1 Approach for the sidehill lie with the ball above the feet.

UNEVEN LIES

When the ground is not level, a player will often face a shot that demands imagination. The ball may land in a number of undesirable positions such as on a hilly lie or under or too close to a tree. You need to know how to play from these situations with confidence. Again, this confidence can only be achieved through practice and gaining an understanding of the trajectory of the ball from these different lies.

Courses vary in terrain and layout. One of the dynamic and refreshing challenges of golf is to adapt to unusual situations with confidence. The most common situations on a hilly course will demand dealing with three types of lies: a sidehill lie, an uphill lie, and a downhill lie. You must make adjustments to your normal setup and swing for each new lie. The sidehill lie, for example, may have the ball above or below your feet.

SIDEHILL LIE: BALL ABOVE YOUR FEET

On a sidehill lie if the ball is above your feet, begin by shortening the grip and leaning into the hill. Place the ball in the center of your stance. Flex your knees slightly, with your weight on the balls of your feet (see figure 12-1). Swing within

FIGURE 12-2 Approach for the sidehill lie with the ball below your feet.

yourself and shorten the backswing; balance is a priority. The ball will tend to draw, that is, ball flight is from right to left for a right-handed golfer and left to right for a left-handed golfer. You must aim right of the target (reverse for the left-handed golfer) or aim up the hill. Remain in your posture throughout the swing. Use one club less than you would use for the same distance from a flat lie because the ball has a tendency to draw; it will roll farther.

SIDEHILL LIE: BALL BELOW YOUR FEET

On a sidehill lie if the ball is below your feet, begin by gripping the top of the club and leaning into the hill. Your weight is toward your heels (see figure 12-2). Swing within yourself and shorten your backswing because balance is a priority. Maintain your posture throughout the swing. Aim to the left of the target (reverse for the left-handed golfer) or slightly up the hill. The ball flight is from left to right for the right-handed golfer and right to left for the left-handed golfer. Use one club more than you would use for the same distance from a flat lie because the ball has a tendency to fade.

FIGURE 12-3 Approach for the uphill lie. The ball is played forward in the stance or on the high side.

FIGURE 12-4 With a downhill lie lean into the hill with your body weight favoring the hill side.

UPHILL LIE

On an uphill lie, grip down the shaft and play the ball forward in the stance or on the high side. Narrow the stance. Lean into the hill, allowing your weight to favor the hilly side (see figure 12-3). Use extra club; if the 9 iron is the club you usually use from this distance, take an 8 iron to compensate for the uphill lie. Swing along the slope of the terrain and remain in posture. An uphill shot has a tendency to go left, so aim to the right of the target. The left-handed golfer will aim left. Swing within yourself; maintaining balance is a priority.

DOWNHILL LIE

On a downhill lie, grip down the shaft and play the ball back in the stance or on the hill side. Widen the stance. Lean into the hill, with your weight favoring the hill side (see figure 12-4). Use more loft and less club. If an 8 iron is the club you usually use for this distance from a flat lie, take a 9 iron because of the downhill. Swing along the slope of the terrain. Maintain your posture. Aim left of target; a

Performance Tip

Checklist for Hilly Lies

1. Swing with the slope.
2. Adjust alignment for hilly lies.
3. Use less club for ball above your feet or a downhill lie.
4. Use more club for ball below your feet or an uphill lie.
5. Swing within yourself.

downhill shot has a tendency to go right. The left-handed golfer should aim right. Again, swing within yourself because maintaining balance is a priority.

PUNCH SHOT

Most golfers at one time or another have to play an attacking shot from under tree branches. You may play safe and chip out to the side, but if you learn to execute a low shot under the branches, you will save strokes. Called a **punch shot** this shot may also be used into a wind. Use a less lofted club than normal. No club above a 7 iron should be used for this shot. You may need to play two clubs more than normal for the same distance. Use your normal grip, but choke down on the grip. Use a square stance and play the ball back in the stance toward the rear foot. Place a little more weight towards the target side foot. Use a closed club face and keep your hands ahead of the ball at address. Swing within yourself low and close to the ground and follow-through.

WIND

Golfers need to know how to make adjustments for wind. The best approach is to grip down the club for more control.

HEAD WIND (INTO THE WIND)

When golfing into a head wind, grip down on club (see figure 12-5). Use more club than normal with a light grip and a square stance. Close the club face and play the ball back in the stance. Shorten the backswing and follow-through low. Be sure to swing with the regular tempo and tee the ball lower (see figure 12-6).

FIGURE 12-5 When hitting into a tail or head wind grip down on the club for more control.

FIGURE 12-6 Teeing your ball higher when playing with a tail wind will usually add distance to your shot. Teeing your ball lower when hitting into a head wind will help keep your shot from gaining loft and losing distance.

TAIL WIND (WIND BEHIND)

When golfing with a tail wind, grip down the shaft (see figure 12-5) with a normal grip and square the club face. You may need less club than normal. Play the ball forward in a square stance. Make a normal swing with a high follow-through. Tee the ball higher and swing with a regular tempo (see figure 12-6).

▶ **Punch Shot**
Using a less lofted club for an attacking low shot from under tree branches or when playing into the wind.

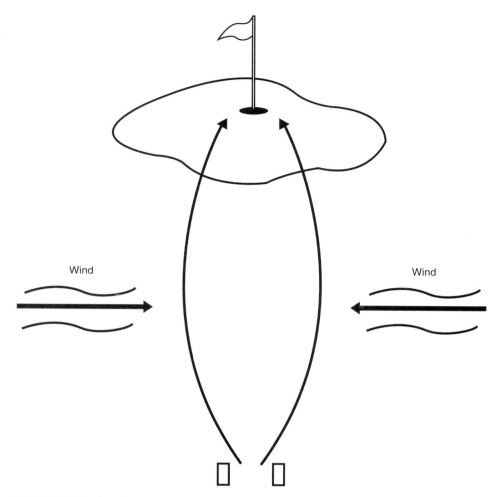

FIGURE 12-7 When hitting into a left or right wind adjust your aim and let the wind carry your ball toward the target.

CROSSWIND

For a left to right crosswind, aim a little left of the target and the wind will take the ball to the flag (reverse for the left-handed golfer). For a right to left crosswind, aim a little right of the target and the wind will take the ball to the flag (reverse for the left-handed golfer) (see figure 12-7).

CURVES IN BALL FLIGHT

Although shots with curving ball flights are common, it can be fun to try to intentionally curve the ball's flight. If you can learn what causes the ball to

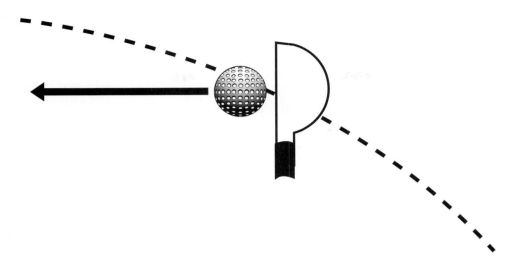

In-to-out swing path

FIGURE 12-8 A draw shot has an in-to-out swing path and results in a long, low shot.

draw or **fade,** you are on your way to correcting yourself when it happens unintentionally.

DRAW (IN-TO-OUT SWING PATH)

The ball's curvature is right to left (reverse for the left-handed golfer) with an in-to-out swing path. A draw flies farther and the ball travels farther in the wind. Draw travels farther and lower than a fade due to the club face being closed at impact.

Use a slightly closed stance or a stronger grip for this shot. You will need a strong grip with your rear hand toward the rear side. You will see three knuckles on the target hand. Setup with the ball toward the toe of the club. Swing the club back more to the inside of the intended target line. This grip takes the club back slightly closed and at impact spins the ball (see figure 12-8). Advanced golfers

▶ **Draw**
A shot with an in-to-out swing path and ball curvature from the right to left (reverse for a left-handed golfer). This shot typically travels far and low due to a closed club face at impact.

▶ **Fade**
A shot with an out-to-in swing path resulting in ball curvature from left to right (reverse for a left-handed golfer). This type of shot has a slightly open club face at impact and flies higher and stops earlier than the draw.

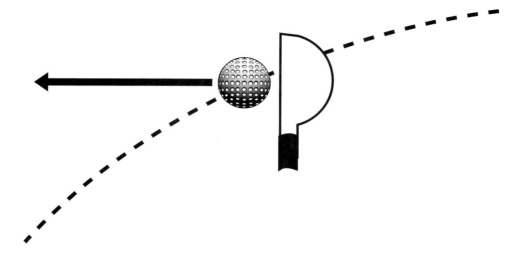

Out-to-in swing path

FIGURE 12-9 A fade has an out-to-in swing path and will give you more loft and less distance than a draw.

need to make only two adjustments—swinging from in to out and striking the ball at a point on the inside of the ball relative to seven o'clock on a clock. (For left handers, relate the striking area to five o'clock on the clock.)

FADE (OUT-TO-IN SWING PATH)

On a fade, the ball curvature is left to right for the right-handed golfer (reverse for the left-handed golfer). The ball flies higher than for the draw and stops earlier. Adapt a slightly open stance or use a weaker grip. Turn hands more to target side (weak grip). This grip takes the club face away slightly open (see figure 12-9). Swing the club back more to the outside of the intended line of flight. The slightly open stance will cause this swing path. A more experienced golfer can usually fade the ball by holding the club face up through impact, rather than turning the face over. By eliminating the rotation of nontarget over the target arm, the face of the club comes slightly across the ball. Short weak slices are caused by taking the club back too far on the inside. This causes the golfer to lead back into the ball with the rear shoulder leaving the club head outside the line of flight (over the top). Remember that overemphasis will cause hooks or slices.

DRILLS FOR HILLY LIES

Tempo and balance should be a priority when playing on hilly lies.

BALANCE AND TEMPO DRILL

Skill Development: Hilly Lies (Balance and Tempo)
Levels: Beginner, Intermediate, Advanced
Start Position: For balance and tempo swing with your feet together.
Evaluation: Hit from the slope, you should strike the ball solid because you are in perfect balance. If the results are inconsistent, return to the drill.

BALANCE ON ONE LEG DRILL

Skill Development: Hilly lies (Balance)
Levels: Beginner, Intermediate, Advanced
Start Position: For balance, hit balls from one leg only. Place the toe of the second leg touching the ground behind you.
Evaluation: Hit from the hilly lie using a compact swing and finish in balance. If you feel your weight on the target side on the follow-through you are improving. Otherwise, return to the Balance and Tempo Drill.

BALANCE FOR A COMPACT SWING DRILL

Skill Development: Hilly Lies (Balance)
Levels: Beginner, Intermediate, Advanced
Start Position: For balance, swing and hold the follow-through.
Evaluation: This drill enables you to make a compact swing necessary for balance on hilly lies. Hit balls from the hilly lie holding the follow-through. You have improved if you finish in balance. If the results have not improved, revert to the drill.

TEMPO TO ELIMINATE OVERSWING DRILL

Skill Development: Hilly Lies (Tempo)
Levels: Beginner, Intermediate, Advanced
Start Position: For tempo, make a full swing with half the speed.
Evaluation: This drill eliminates overswinging, and a swing that is too fast. Make your normal swing on the hilly lie and see if the tempo is better.
Skill Development: Hilly Lies (Tempo)
Levels: Beginner, Intermediate, Advanced
Start Position: Make swings on hilly lies using plastic balls.
Evaluation: Use regular balls; you should feel more balanced. If this drill does not help, revert to the Balance and Tempo Drill.

PRACTICE

Introduce your practice of twenty-five repetitions—grip, align/aim, and setup. Here is a practice program.

1. Practice with plastic balls until you feel comfortable with the setup.
2. Practice on relevant hills using clubs on the ground for the setup.
3. Practice on relevant hills setup directly at the target and observe the results. Make the adjustments and observe the results. Repeat this practice until the setup is automatic.
4. If hilly terrain is not available, adapt the facility to create a hilly lie. Use two 2″ × 4″ boards on top of each other, or place your foot (target or rear depending on the lie required) on an upturned bucket.

SUMMARY

- When playing the ball from a hilly lie remember to swing with the slope, adjust your alignment appropriately, and use less club for a ball above your feet or on a downhill lie and more club for a ball below your feet or on an uphill lie.
- Learning to execute a punch shot will help you when hitting from beneath trees or into the wind and shave strokes off your game.
- When hitting into a crosswind aim slightly to the left or right of the target (depending on the direction of the wind) and let the wind bring the ball back on target.
- Learning to intentionally cause a ball to draw or fade will assist you in correcting this problem when it occurs unintentionally.

CHAPTER 13

CONDITIONING:
PHYSICAL AND MENTAL

OBJECTIVES

After reading this chapter, you should be able to do the following:

- Understand the importance of conditioning for golf.
- Know why it is essential to practice fitness of the mind and the body.
- Adapt relaxation techniques to improve your game.
- Practice a positive attitude to make yourself a winner.

KEY TERMS

While reading this chapter, you will become familiar with the following terms:

- ▶ **Aerobic Fitness Activity**
- ▶ **Relaxation Technique**

PHYSICAL CONDITIONING

Golf combines fun, nature, and exercise. To get the full exercise benefit from golf you should walk the course every chance you get; even better, carry your bag. Golf is a good workout. You will gain some muscle tone in the shoulders, back, forearms, and legs. Golf does not strengthen the heart enough to consider it an **aerobic fitness activity,** and because many golfers use motorized carts, an aerobic program would be to their benefit. A stronger heart equals a longer life, which equals more time to enjoy golf. When a person is physically fit that person can cope with the general activities of everyday life and still have enough energy left to enjoy leisure activities. Research has shown that aerobically fit individuals increase in productivity. When a person is aerobically fit, they use more oxygen, so energy gets to the working muscles without much effort. A golfer, like any athlete, should work on an endurance, strength, and a muscular-flexibility program.

AEROBIC FITNESS

Everyone should develop a cardiovascular fitness program to strengthen their heart muscle. Like all other muscles in the body, the heart must be overloaded to build and strengthen. Developing a stronger heart muscle means your heart pumps less and you experience less fatigue. When a golfer is aerobically fit, he or she can cope with the physical demands of 18 holes. Being less fatigued makes it easier to maintain a consistent swing and tempo. Not distracted by fatigue, the golfer can then concentrate on the mental fitness necessary for a successful 18 holes of golf.

All golfers should participate in some form of cardiovascular endurance exercise for at least twenty minutes three to five times each week. Studies from the Aerobic Institute show that exercising for shorter periods a few times a day is also beneficial. Some examples of cardiovascular exercises are fast walking, jogging, rope skipping, cycling, using a stairmaster, aerobicizing, and cross-country skiing.

STRENGTH TRAINING

A strength program will benefit the golfer by strengthening the muscles necessary for power. Strength programs help increase lean body tissue and increase metabolism. A golfer developing muscular strength must be aware of the major golfing muscles. These are the legs, back, shoulders, neck, and arms. The necessity for flexibility, especially in the upper body, means it is important not to overbuild, particularly the chest muscles. Seek the assistance of an instructor in the strength-

▶ **Aerobic Fitness Activity**
Activities that increase cardiovascular fitness and strengthen the heart. People with high levels of aerobic fitness can easily cope with the physical demands of daily life, have increased productivity, and more energy for leisure activities.

training program at a university or a trainer at a health club. They will advise you on frequency, intensity, and adequate rest between workouts needed for recovery.

FLEXIBILITY

Flexibility allows the joints to move freely. A joint's range of motion varies from one individual to another and from joint to joint within the same individual. Anyone can improve their flexibility through a daily program. Flexibility is of utmost importance for the golfer because it assists in the prevention of injuries and aids in performance. The most common sites for injury are the back, wrist, shoulders, elbows, and knees. These require special attention in your flexibility program. Many muscular and skeletal problems, especially in golf, may be related to a lack of flexibility and poor golf mechanics.

Before participating in any form of exercise you should warm up the exercising muscles by walking or jogging. Walking may be best before a round of golf. Continue by stretching the exercising muscles. A slow sustained stretch to the point of mild discomfort is required. Stretch and hold the position for a few seconds. The following exercises could be included in a warm-up program.

1. Aerobic exercise—walk, jog, or skip.
2. Flexibility exercise moving through all parts of the body from the head to the feet.
3. Hit a few balls with each club. If time does not allow you to get to the practice range, swing a weighted club. Swing a club in the right hand only and then the left hand only. Always repeat the stretching program after a round of golf.

FLEXIBILITY EXERCISES

1. Lateral Head Movement (head, neck, spine): Slowly move your head from side to side (see figure 13-1).

FIGURE 13-1 Lateral Head Movement. Slowly moving the head from side-to-side works your head, neck, and spine.

FIGURE 13-2 Arm Circles. Slowly circling your arms in front of you forward and backward helps to loosen up your shoulders.

2. Arm Circles (shoulders): Stretch your arms directly in front of you or out to your sides and slowly circle your arms. Repeat in the opposite direction (see figure 13-2) .

3. Shoulder Stretch (shoulders): Take your left arm and stretch across your chest at shoulder height. Hold your elbow with your right hand. Apply gentle pressure. Repeat on right side (see figure 13-3).

4. Side Stretch (back): Side stretch with your hands on your hips, your feet shoulder width apart. Stretch by moving your upper body to one side and hold the position. Repeat on the other side (see figure 13-4).

5. Body Rotation (back): With your arms out in front and bent, rotate your body as far as possible and hold the position. Repeat on the other side (see figure 13-5).

6. Back and Leg Stretch (back, legs): Stand and cross your right leg in front of your left leg; bend over and reach towards

FIGURE 13-3 Shoulder Stretch. Hold the elbow with the opposite hand and apply gentle pressure.

the ground. Feel the stretch on your lower back and hamstrings. It is not wise to cross your legs if you suffer from back problems (see figure 13-6).

FIGURE 13-4 Side Stretch. Hands on hips, feet shoulder width apart.

FIGURE 13-5 Body Rotation. With your arms out in front of you and bent at a 90 degree angle rotate the body as far as possible from left to right and then back from right to left.

FIGURE 13-6 Back and Leg Stretch. You should feel the stretch on the lower back and hamstrings.

7. Squeeze a Squash Ball (hands, arms): Squeeze the ball in your right hand and then in your left hand.
8. Roll the Cord (hands, arms): Put a weight on the end of a cord tied to a ruler. Hold the ruler in both hands, palms facing downwards with arms outstretched at shoulder height. Wind the weight up and down by coiling and uncoiling the cord on the ruler.
9. Arm Drill with Club (forearm, wrist): Arm at side bend at elbow. Place a club in the hand, clubhead and shaft pointing toward the sky. Rotate the forearm to the right and then to the left.

These are but a few of the numerous exercises that will benefit the golfer. Invent your own program to suit your needs. Do exercises that work the major golf muscles; hold the stretch for a few seconds and repeat ten times. Remember you are not trying to prepare for a marathon, but by preparing the body and mind, you will enjoy a lifetime sport for a lifetime!

MENTAL CONDITIONING

Physical and mental health go hand in hand. If you feel good about yourself physically you are well on the road to a better quality of life and total well-being. Mental well-being is an important component of total well-being. Like physical health it must be practiced to reach full potential.

GOLF IS MENTAL

After you have mastered the skills of the game, golf is between the ears. In order to make mental toughness a habit, you need to learn how to cope with stressful situations on and off the golf course. The golfer with great concentration will perform better than the golfer with superior golfing ability and a negative attitude. Too often golfers who are on the course for relaxation begin to lose control and succumb to stress. To improve this situation, there are a number of **relaxation techniques** that can be practiced before and during a round of golf. You should pick the one or two that are most suited to your personality.

RELAXATION TECHNIQUE

1. Deep breathing: Concentrate on breathing away the tension. Breathe in; slowly inhale through your nose and exhale through your mouth. Repeat the exercise eight to ten times. You may also apply this method on the course and take a deep breath before a shot.
2. Stretching: Stretch going through your entire body from your head to your toes. Stretch and hold. Use this method to relax a certain area of your body before a shot.

3. Muscle relaxation: Feel the tension in your body by tightening, then relaxing. This exercise should be performed at home on the floor, and work through the major muscle groups. Become tense, then relax, and hold the contraction for about six seconds, then go limp (relax). Note the different feeling.
4. Meditation: Concentrate on a word, a phrase, or breathing. Sit in a comfortable chair and in your mind repeat the word or phrase you have chosen. This helps you clear your mind and block out all worries. You may also listen to a relaxation tape, such as soothing music. Perform this technique for approximately twenty minutes in a quiet room. You could perform this in the locker room before going to the course.
5. Visualization: Sit in a quiet place and visualize the 18 holes of golf, or visualize how you will play each hole or shot. Visualize your own swing or maybe even a swing you admire. Take this visualization onto the golf course with you. In order to use imagery on the course it must be practiced off the course.

CONFIDENCE

To be successful in life or in sport requires a good deal of self-confidence. If you have prepared yourself for the game and are realistic about your golfing ability, your performance will be enhanced through the practice of relaxation techniques combined with a positive attitude. Winners believe in themselves and trust their ability. The techniques mentioned previously will keep you physically and mentally relaxed. You will be more in control and better able to concentrate on the task ahead.

CONCENTRATION

Concentration is the focusing of the mind and the body on the task. It takes a strong mind to concentrate fully for a complete round of golf, which could last up to four hours. You must be able to concentrate for each shot and then take time to enjoy the company and the beauty of the surroundings between shots. It is important to develop and incorporate an identical preshot routine for every shot. This routine will help the golfer when under pressure. The mental or positive part of this routine will not be obvious to others, but it plays a major part in golfing success. Paint positive pictures, feel relaxed over the ball (grip relaxed, shoulders relaxed, and setup relaxed), and visualize the ball flight as well as the result. The

▶ **Relaxation Techniques**
Controlling thought processes to effectively manage stress.

technique of imagery must be practiced off and on the golf course in order to improve. Rehearse the process and the outcome of every shot. Every visualization must be positive; you can groove your swing by repeating it in your mind. A good swing is one that is repeatable every time, especially under pressure.

ATTITUDE

Golf must be fun for you and your playing partners. Remove yourself from any concepts about golf being pressure filled. Do not waste energy on negative thoughts. Use all your energy in a positive way. Try not to be intimidated by another player's ability. Play within yourself and stay tough. Take your time; be patient. It is permissible to play a bad shot; just don't dwell on it and anchor the good ones. If you are experiencing a bad day, do not complain or focus on your round at the expense of destroying your playing partner's game. Whatever the outcome, you should be able to say, "I did my very best on every shot, and that was the best golf and score that I could return today." Remember, what you put into life, you get out of it. You must believe that you are a winner. Your attitude could be the difference between your success or failure.

SUMMARY

- To get the best physical results from a round of golf, walk the course whenever you can. This also allows you the opportunity to fully appreciate the surrounding landscape.
- Golfers should partake in aerobic fitness and strength and flexibility training to reduce their experience of fatigue and ensure a strong, full range of motion.
- After mastering the physical skills of the game, the most important games are won or lost in the golfer's mind. Relaxation techniques, focusing on good shots and sound effort, and incorporating a consistent preshot routine are beneficial in helping the golfer avoid many of the mental pitfalls.
- Confidence, concentration, and a positive attitude will make any outing, regardless of playing level and skill, one that can be enjoyable.

CHAPTER 14

SETTING GOALS: PHYSICAL AND MENTAL

OBJECTIVES

After reading this chapter, you should be able to do the following:

- Realize that all goals need to be realistic.
- Understand the importance of physical and mental goals for improving your golf.

KEY TERM

While reading this chapter, you will become familiar with the following terms:

► **Confidence Builder**

GOAL SETTING

Be realistic about your physical ability. You must set goals that are achievable. Do not set goals so high that you do not feel any achievement. Goals that are realistic enable you to believe in yourself and your ability. Take time to look at all aspects of your game; find your strengths and weaknesses. By doing this you will be able to set a program for the off-season where you can work on your weaknesses and your strengths. This is a wonderful **confidence builder.** Once you have set realistic goals and put in the practice required to achieve them you can expect to perform well. Good performance boosts confidence and self-esteem.

PHYSICAL AND MENTAL GOAL SETTING

Remember to follow the A, B, C, and D of physical and mental goal setting. Be sure to make your goals: Achievable, Believable, Controllable, and Desirable.

ACHIEVABLE

Once you are realistic about your physical ability you can set an achievable goal. If your skill level does not warrant a gross 72 and you continue to try to achieve that goal, you will lose heart quickly when you do not achieve a 72. It would be far more realistic to say, "I will improve my handicap by three strokes this year."

BELIEVABLE

You must believe in your own ability. If you are an excellent chipper, you must believe that you can get up and down at least three times in a round. You chip from off the green, the ball stops close to the hole, and you one putt.

CONTROLLABLE

You are in control of your game preparation. Take note of game preparation and not the golf swing. People are attracted to the game because it appears controllable. The only thing you are in control of is you. You can control your physical and mental practice program. Control your golf preparation: (1) exercise three times a week, (2) practice the physical skills three times a week, and (3) practice the mental skills three times a week.

DESIRABLE

Sometimes people try to achieve too much. Perhaps a coach has been working with you on a regular basis and is excited about your game. Remove yourself from outside pressures. Concentrate on pleasing yourself, not others, with your performance.

PHYSICAL GOAL SETTING

1. Practice skills on the range.
2. Learn the rules; they may work in your favor.
3. Practice your weaknesses. (Perhaps your bunker play or hilly lies).
4. Practice preshot routine.
5. Practice the twenty-five Swing Drill.
6. Practice aerobic conditioning.
7. Bring your game to the course.

Set these physical goals for the year, month, week, round, hole, and shot:

YEAR: Lower handicap by three strokes.

MONTH: Practice hilly lies.

WEEK: Go to the course twice and practice on the range twice.

ROUND: Play with the swing you bring to the golf course.

HOLE: Remain focused; concentrate on the task at hand; do not dwell or brood on the last hole.

SHOT: Use your preshot routine; play the lie first, the obstacle second, and the distance last.

MENTAL GOAL SETTING

Once you build your confidence through practicing skills, you also need to practice relaxation techniques for coping with stress and emotions. Golf does produce stress. Playing bad affects the ego. Golf is an amazing game in that most people are so involved in their own game that they never notice the perceived problems of another golfer.

► **Confidence Builder**

A training program that works on your weaknesses and your strengths will give you noticeable results that boost performance, confidence, and self-esteem.

Everyone feels stress on the course. Coping strategies are essential for dealing with it. Be positive and reinforce that positive feeling with positive self-talk such as "Good shot," "That's the way," or "What a shot!" Anchor each good shot and forget the bad shots. Paint positive pictures and practice visualization. Visualize the ball landing in optimum positions. Rehearse the process and outcome of every shot through imagery. Practice relaxation techniques.

Set your mental goals for the year, month, week, round, hole and shot:

YEAR: Practice twenty minutes of meditation every day.

MONTH: Once a month practice imagery at home. In order to bring this to the course, it must be practiced at home. Close your eyes and play each hole in your mind.

WEEK: Have fun; don't take yourself too seriously.

ROUND: Only have positive thoughts. Negative thoughts waste energy and detract from performance.

HOLE: Learn how to take one hole at a time; play within your ability and stay tough.

SHOT: Do your preshot routine and visualize the ball flight and result of every shot. Take only one shot at a time.

Keep a journal of your goals and your achievements. Reevaluate your goals periodically. You may have underestimated your ability.

SUMMARY

- Following the A, B, C, and D of physical and mental goal setting will help you plan a course of action that is Achievable, Believable, Controllable, and Desirable.
- To bring your best game to the course, practice your skills on the range, learn the rules, practice your preshot routine, practice the twenty-five Swing Drill, and incorporate aerobic conditioning into your training program.
- Goal setting and achievement is a process of building on a series of successes. Set your physical and mental goals by the year, month, week, round, hole, and shot.
- Keeping a journal of your goals and achievements will help you reevaluate your goals. Periodic review of this journal may surprise you. Don't underestimate your ability!

CHAPTER 15

MANAGING **YOUR GAME** ON THE COURSE

OBJECTIVES

After reading this chapter, you should be able to do the following:

- Learn what it takes to play a winning game.
- Understand the value of playing positive golf on the good days and the bad days.
- Realize that each hole and round should be planned ahead.
- Explain why the golfer should never give up.

KEY TERMS

While reading this chapter, you will become familiar with the following terms:

- ▶ **Dogleg**
- ▶ **Getting Up and Down from Off the Green**
- ▶ **Regulation**

COURSE MANAGEMENT

Many golfers have the perfect swing and the perfect game on the driving range, and somehow it leaves them on the golf course. Here, I remind you again of the reply from the university team member when questioned by her coach about a new member's golf game. "Coach, she plays great golf on the range, but her game don't travel."

KNOW YOUR GAME

All players need to be familiar enough with their own game to identify their strengths and weaknesses. Years ago, all players played through feel. There were no yardage markers. Players looked at the target, determined it was a 5 iron, took out the club, and hit the shot. No longer. All good professionals and amateurs know how far they hit each club and use the yardage markers on the course to help them with club selection.

Practice with each club at the range and pace out the yardage. If it is not realistic to pace the yardage for all of your clubs maybe just use your 7 iron, hit ten or twelve shots, and take the average. Assume that the distance between each club is approximately ten yards. Through quality practice the golfer will learn the distance they can expect to hit each club. Keep a record of your yardage where you can consult it (see table 15-1). The player should keep a record of their most recent scores, maybe the last twelve rounds. The player can see how consistent or inconsistent their game is (see table 15-2). Also keep a record of drives in the fairway, shots on the green in regulation, up and down from off the green or from a bunker, and the number of putts for the round (see table 15-3).

Regulation implies that allowing two putts per green, the ball lands on the par 3 in one shot, on the par 4 in two shots, and on the par 5 in three shots. **Getting up and down from off the green** implies that the ball did not land on the green in regulation, but the pitch, chip, or bunker shot landed close enough to the flag and you one putted. Understand your scorecard and be aware that the numbers under the handicap column on the scorecard identify the difficulty of each hole. A handicap of one is the most difficult hole and a handicap of 18 is the easiest hole on that course. Review the card before playing the round (see figure 15-1).

▶ **Regulation**
Allows for two putts per hole, assuming that on a par 3 hole the golfer lands on the green in one shot, on a par 4 hole they land on the green in two, and on a par 5 they land on the green in three.

▶ **Getting Up and Down from Off the Green**
Getting up and down from off the green means that the ball didn't land on the green in regulation, but that the pitch or chip landed close enough to the hole to one putt it.

TABLE 15-1
Yardage Chart

Club	My Average
1 Driver	
3 Wood	
5 Wood	
7 Iron	
2 Iron	
3 Iron	
4 Iron	
5 Iron	
6 Iron	
7 Iron	
8 Iron	
9 Iron	
Pitch	
Sand Wedge	

TABLE 15-2
Graph of Last Ten Rounds

	1	2	3	4	5	6	7	8	9	10
125										
120										
115										
110										
105										
100										
95										
90										
85										
80										
75										
70										

TABLE 15-3
Game Analysis

Hole	Par	Your Score	Drive in Fairway	Greens Hit in Regulation	Chip Pitch Sand	Number of Putts
1						
2						
3						
4						
5						
6						
7						
8						
9						
10						
11						
12						
13						
14						
15						
16						
17						
18						

HOLE NO.	1	2	3	4	5	6	7	8	9	Out	10	11	12	13	14	15	16	17	18	In	Total	HDCP	Net
GOLD	291	175	360	211	387	343	399	520	524	3210	144	512	409	490	387	378	361	149	374	3204	6414		
WHITE	278	161	315	200	371	327	383	506	509	3050	131	503	359	473	364	366	347	136	364	3043	6093		
MEN'S HDCP	15	17	13	9	1	11	3	5	7		16	8	4	6	2	10	12	18	14				
PAR	4	3	4	3	4	4	4	5	5	36	3	5	4	5	4	4	4	3	4	36	72		
RED	267	147	305	139	292	315	342	468	434	2709	118	426	301	411	338	294	339	120	356	2703	5412		
WOMEN'S HDCP	13	15	7	17	11	9	5	1	3		18	2	12	4	6	14	10	16	8				

Slope Rating: Red-113   Course Rating: Red-69.9

DATE   SCORER   ATTEST

FIGURE 15-1 Sample scorecard.

PLAY WITH THE SWING YOU BRING TO THE COURSE

If you have prepared yourself well physically and mentally, you must believe in yourself and in your abilities. The swing you bring to the course one day may be different from the swing the previous day or the one you had on the driving range. You must accept it and play with it.

Remember it is not how well you look, how well you swing, or how far you can hit the ball that matters. Believe it or not, it is how you score. Your objective is to play the course and get the ball into the hole in as few shots as possible. You must visualize and think about each hole and each shot. Realize that each shot carries the same value whether it is a drive of 200 yards or a one inch putt. Follow your identical preshot routine for each shot, and do not become complacent.

MATCH PLAY AND STROKE PLAY

As stated in chapter 4 there are many different types of competition, but stroke play (medal) and match play (hole-by-hole) are the most popular. Both require you to play the course. If you play the course better than the opponent in match play you will win. If you play match play by waiting to plan your strategy by the other players' mistakes, you could be very disappointed.

Play positively and attack the course. From the moment you go onto the first tee, whether stroke play or match play, you must plan ahead. Play your game; do not be intimidated by other players' shot length or ability. Even if you are playing with an accomplished player, enjoy the experience and pay attention. In golf there is always an opportunity to learn.

PICKING A TARGET

Remember to pick your target for every shot and follow your game plan. Decide how you will play the hole from the tee by picking out a definite target. Your target cannot be just down the middle or down the left, not just the white house, or the mountain in the distance. Pick a specific spot. Be determined to land the ball there. Be aware of where the hazards are and play away from them. Play the percentage shot. If the hole is a **dogleg,** where it goes to the right or the left

▶ **Dogleg**
   The fairway angles to the right or the left, identified as a dogleg right or dogleg left.

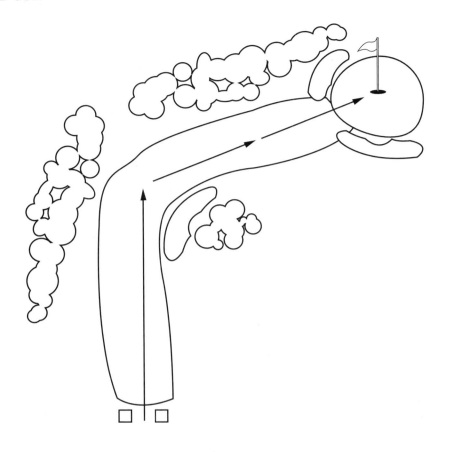

Dogleg right

FIGURE 15-2 Decide on the tee the most productive way to play each hole.

(see figure 15-2), decide on the tee the most productive way to play it. Beware of the cross bunker; if you hit the perfect drive you will carry them and reach the green in two.

What if you hit a not-so-perfect drive? It may be in your best interest to play a 3 wood from the tee and land short of the bunker. You may also need to make adjustments in club selection for weather conditions. The course may be saturated with water or there may be a strong wind. A tail wind or head wind could mean a 1, 2, or 3 club difference in either direction.

KEEP THE BALL IN PLAY

You should try to play safe. Do not go for the shot of the day. More often than not when it doesn't come off it will cost you more strokes. To keep the ball in play if you are in the deep rough and a 3 iron distance from the green, be sure to consider your lie first. Maybe you need to play the 7 iron, which has more loft, to get the ball back in the fairway. If you are in the middle of pine trees with no shot to the green and no way out, do not try to play the miracle shot to the green. Play out to the side—the safe shot! When you try the miracle shot and it does not come off, your thinking becomes distorted and you begin to lose composure.

When you feel yourself beginning to lose composure it is time to use your relaxation technique (maybe a few deep breaths) to regain your calm and confidence. Stop and take a moment to reorganize and visualize the shot you want to make and the result. If you had visualized that miracle shot you would never have played it. Do not allow one error to add up to two or three more shots. When you find yourself in trouble accept that you may have to play safe at the cost of one stroke and continue with your original game plan. Never allow a few bad shots to become a few bad holes. A golfer's greatest fear is failing. The sooner that we accept that we are human and it is all right to make mistakes, a bad shot or bad swing, and get on with it, our games will improve.

BEWARE OF TERRAIN AND CONDITIONS

It is important to adjust your game to the playing conditions. As mentioned earlier, wind and rain will affect your club selection and possibly the type of shot played. Evaluation of the terrain will also determine which club to use. If the terrain is very hilly careful adjustments must be made for each shot. Facing an uphill shot may require an extra club. The same applies to a downhill shot. These shots will necessitate less club than for the same distance on flat terrain.

You also need to be aware of adjustments in setup (see discussion on uneven lies). If you are playing a parkland course with a number of trees it is important to play the lie first, the obstacle second (trajectory), and the distance last. It is easy to look at the lie and the distance and forget to take the carry of the trees into account. After taking the trees into consideration you may have to decide on a more lofted club and be satisfied to play just short of the green.

GO PAST THE FLAG

Often golfers leave their approach shots short of the flag. It is your responsibility to know the pin placement and length of the green. The pin may have a plastic ball or tiny flag close to the bottom, center, or high up identifying the position of the hole on the green, which implies the hole is in the front, middle, or at the back of the green. While playing each hole the golfer should become familiar with pin placements on adjacent greens. The length of the green may vary from twenty-five yards to forty yards. This could be the difference of two or three clubs.

If you are deciding between a 9 iron or a 8 iron try the 8 iron. Take the risk of landing past the flag. Keep a record next time of how often you are past the flag on an approach shot. You will be surprised. You will find you are short more often than you are long. Give yourself a chance. When you are unsure of the club selection, go with your gut feeling; it is usually right.

TROUBLE IN FRONT AND BEHIND THE GREEN

Beware of any trouble in front and behind the green. If the entrance to the green is surrounded by bunkers it may be in your best interest to take an extra club and play safe. For instance the golfer would take a 7 iron rather than the shorter 8 iron. The opposite may also apply if the back of the green is surrounded by trees or has a deep fall away from the green. In this case you would want to play short.

Choosing the appropriate club is important. Choose the shorter club if there is (1) trouble behind the green, (2) a tail wind (wind behind), (3) a downhill lie, (4) you have a tendency to draw, or (5) the ground is hard. Choose the longer club if there is (1) trouble in front of the green, (2) a head wind (into the wind), (3) an uphill lie, (4) you have a tendency to fade or slice, or (5) the ground is soft.

READING THE GREEN

Do not wait until you reach the green to begin reading it. Start reading the green as you walk toward it. Observe the surrounding terrain, water, mountains, or hills. You usually find a putt will run toward the water or fall away from a mountain or a hill. Do your homework before you reach the green. On the green observe your partner's putt, and learn from it.

Observe your own putt from four positions. Look at the putt from behind the ball, from the other side of the hole, and from right and left of the line of the putt. Ask yourself a few questions. Is the green fast or slow? A fast green is usually shiny and the grass grows away from you. A slow green is dull with the grass growing toward you. Is the ground soft and wet? Is it an uphill or downhill putt? Answer these questions, perform your preshot routine, and make your stroke. Visualize it into the hole.

NEVER GIVE UP

Everyone experiences good days and bad days on and off the golf course. Do not allow anger or self-pity to enter your life or game. It would be great to hit four beautiful shots to the par 4, but four ugly shots give the same score. Winners are tough. Learn from your mistakes. Be patient; you are allowed to play a bad round. Keep a positive attitude.

No one will wish to play with you if you cry about every shot or continue to complain about the last hole where you had an eight. Do not spoil the opposition's game. They came to relax. You will become a better golfer and a wonderful human being if you are humble in victory and gracious in defeat.

Golf is fun and should be played with that attitude. Even bad golf can be fun!

SUMMARY

- Knowing how far you can hit each club along with using the yardage markers on the course will assist in proper club selection.
- Each shot carries the same value whether a drive of 200 yards or a one inch putt.
- Pick your target for each shot, and be determined to land the ball there. Deciding on the tee the most productive way to play a hole can keep you out of the rough or a hazard.
- A good golfer knows their limits and when to take chances. Sometimes the safe shot that doesn't carry as far or simply gets you back onto the fairway will actually be better than the miracle shot.
- Play the lie first, the obstacle second, and the distance last.
- Read each putt from four directions: behind the ball, from the other side of the hole, and from the right and left of the line of the putt. Use these perspectives to determine the nature of the green and adjust accordingly.
- Remember, even bad golf can be fun!

Appendix A

There are many terms used on the golf course, and all students of golf should familiarize themselves with the proper terminology.

ACE: A hole in one.

ADDRESS THE BALL: Taking your stance and grounding the club, (except in a hazard,) before you swing. In a hazard a player has addressed the ball when the stance has been taken.

ALL SQUARE: The term used to indicate that the match is even in match play.

APPROACH: A shot played to the putting green.

APRON: Grass area surrounding the putting green (fringe).

AWAY: Ball farthest from the hole is played first.

BACK NINE: The last nine holes of an 18 hole course; also called "In."

BACKSWING: When the club is swung away from the ball, up to the rear shoulder.

BALL MARK: The mark made on the green when a ball lands. It should be repaired with a tee or repair tool and then tapped down with the putter.

BIRDIE: One below par for a given hole.

BOGEY: One over par for a given hole.

BREAK: The shape of the putting green. The putt breaks to the right or the left, depending on the slope.

BUNKER: A hazard covered with sand. Often called a "trap" or a "sand trap." Grass bordering or within the bunker is not considered part of the bunker.

CADDIE: The person who carries the player's clubs. A caddie may give the player advice.

CASUAL WATER: A temporary accumulation of water on the course from rain or sprinklers. One may remove the ball or their feet from these areas without penalty.

CHIP: A stroke made from just off the green that has more roll time than air time.

CLOSED: The position of the feet on the ground or the lie of the club face in relation to the target. If the feet are aimed right or the club face is turned to the left, they are considered closed (reverse for the left-handed golfer).

CUP: Another term used for the hole.

DIVOT: The turf displaced by the club when swinging. You should replace the divot and tap down the ground with your foot or the club.

DOGLEG: The fairway angles to the right or the left, identified as a dogleg right or a dogleg left.

DORMIE: A player or a side in match play is dormie when it is as many holes up as the number of holes left to play: 4 up with 4 holes to play.

DOUBLE BOGEY: Two strokes over par for a given hole.

DOWN: Match play; the number of holes a player is behind.

DRAW: A shot that curves slightly from right to left (reverse for the left-handed golfer). This ball flight has more roll when it lands.

DOWNSWING: The swing from the top of the backswing until impact with the ball.

DRIVER: The longest and least lofted club in the set. This club is used from off the tee and is designed to give the longest length.

EAGLE: Two strokes under par for a given hole.

EXPLOSION SHOT: Played from the sand bunker.

EXECUTIVE COURSE: A golf course slightly shorter than a regulation course. There are some par 4s but mostly par 3s.

FACE: The area on the club head that strikes the ball.

FADE: The ball curves slightly from left to right (reverse for the left-handed golfer). This ball has less roll on landing.

FAIRWAY: The closely mowed area between the teeing ground and the green.

FAT: Hitting the ground behind the ball before striking the ball.

FLAGSTICK: This shows the location of the hole on the green. Also called the "pin."

FOLLOW-THROUGH: The swing from impact down the target line to a high finish, facing the target with the weight on the target side.

FORE: A warning cry. On hearing "Fore!," turn you back and duck your head.

FOURSOME: The most common grouping of players to speed up play. Two players may be grouped with two other players.

FOURBALL: A match in which two golfers play their better ball against the better ball of two other golfers.

FRINGE: The name for the shorter grass surrounding the green; also known as the apron.

FRONT NINE: The first nine holes of an 18 hole course; also called "out."

GIMMIE: In friendly play, a putt that is very close to the hole is conceded by the opponent. You pick the ball up and add the stroke.

GREEN: The putting area.

GROSS SCORE: The total score for the round.

GROUND UNDER REPAIR: White staked or lined area on the golf course where repairs are being done or there are new trees that need protection. It may state "GUR." The ball may be lifted and dropped at the nearest point of relief. If the ground under repair interferes with the stance, relief is also allowed.

GROUNDING THE CLUB: Placing the sole or the flange of the club on the ground in the address position.

HANDICAP: A method used to equate the different abilities of players. Handicap indices are used to equalize players.

HALVED: The same score for each player on a hole in match play competition. A match may also be halved, that is both players won the same number of holes over 18 holes.

HAZARD: The term used for bunkers and water hazards on the course.

HOLE: The four and one-fourth inch hole in the ground on the putting green. Also the complete area from the tee to the green.

HOLE-IN-ONE: Hitting the ball into the hole from the tee shot.

HOLE OUT: To finish the play of the hole by putting or hitting the ball into the cup.

HONOR: The player scoring the lowest on the preceding hole gets the honor. The right to tee off first.

HOOK: Ball flight that curves drastically from right to left (reverse for the left-handed golfer).

HOSEL: The part of the club head that fits into the shaft.

IN THE LEATHER: An informal guideline for conceding a putt. If the putt is no longer than the shaft from the end of the grip to the blade, it is "in the leather" and may be conceded. It is considered a stroke.

LAG PUTT: A long putt that stops close to the hole.

LATERAL WATER HAZARD: Lake, pond, sea, river, or ditch that runs parallel to the line of the hole. It is marked with red stakes or red lines.

LIE: The position of the ball on the ground. The lie of the head of the club on the ground.

LOFT: This is the angle of the face of the club. The driver has the least loft and the sand wedge has the most loft.

LOOSE IMPEDIMENTS: An object such as a twig, branch (not growing), or a leaf. Sand and soil are also considered loose impediments on the green, but not elsewhere. Loose impediments may not be removed from a hazard.

LPGA: Ladies Professional Golf Association. There is a playing division and a teaching division.

MARKER: The ball may be lifted from its position and cleaned while on the putting green. You place a small round object such as a coin behind the ball and then lift the ball. Your opponent may ask you to mark the ball if it is in the line of their putt. Always replace the ball in front of the marker.

MATCH PLAY: In this type of competition, each hole is a separate contest. The winner is the player or team winning the most number of holes.

MEDAL PLAY: This is also known as stroke play.

MOVED: A ball is deemed to have moved if it leaves the original position and comes to rest in another place.

NASSAU: One point is awarded for each nine and one point for the match. Three points are possible.

NET SCORE: The handicap deducted from the gross score.

OPEN: The position of the feet or the club head in relation to the target line. The stance is open if the feet are aimed left of the target. The clubface is open if it is aiming right of the target (reverse for the left-handed golfer).

OPEN TOURNAMENT: Professionals and amateurs may participate. There is normally a prequalifying round.

OUT OF BOUNDS: Ground on which play is prohibited. This area is marked by white stakes. You may not play from out of bounds.

PAR: The standard of scoring for each hole. A par 3, 4, or 5 hole. A par 72 course.

PENALTY STROKE: Added to the score of a player or a side for an infringement.

PGA OF AMERICA: Professional Golfer Association. The association is mostly of men but women are accepted.

PGA TOUR: An association of male players who play on regular tour events.

PITCH: A shot executed with a lofted club, producing a high trajectory and little roll.

PITCH MARK: The mark left on the green from the high-approach shot. These marks should be repaired; it is legal to do so even if the mark is in the line of your putt.

PROVISIONAL BALL: A ball played for a ball that may be lost (not lost in a water hazard) or may be out of bounds. The provisional ball is used to speed up play. It is played from where you hit the last ball and may be played until you reach where the original ball may be lost. If the original is found it must be played provided it is in bounds. Otherwise, the provisional ball is the ball in play.

PULL: A ball traveling left of the target (reverse for the left-handed golfer).

PUSH: A ball traveling right of the target (reverse for the left-handed golfer).

R & A: In conjunction with the United States Golf Association, the Royal and Ancient (R & A), St Andrew's, Scotland, revise the rules of golf.

ROUGH: The long unkept grass bordering the fairway.

RUB OF THE GREEN: A ball in motion accidently stopped or deflected by an outside agency.

SAND TRAP: A bunker that contains sand. The official name is bunker.

SAND WEDGE: This is the most lofted club in the bag.

SCRAMBLE: A competition where the entire team plays one shot from the best position.

SCRATCH: A player who scores par.

SCOTCH FOURSOMES: Two players play as a team using one ball and playing every second shot.

SHAFT: The part of the club made of steel, graphite, boron, or other materials. It is attached to the clubhead.

SHANK: A shot where the ball is hit from the hosel of the club instead of the club face.

SLICE: A ball that flies drastically from left to right (reverse for the left-handed golfer).

SOLE: The part of the club that rests on the ground.

SPIKES: The cleats on the sole of the golf shoe for traction.

SPIKE MARKS: Marks made on the putting green by dragging the feet. If these marks are in the line of the putt, they may not be repaired. Repair the marks on leaving the green.

STANCE: The position of the feet on the ground while addressing the ball.

STARTER: The golf course employee who registers the golfers. You must report in before you tee off.

STROKE: The forward motion of the club with the intention of hitting the ball.

STROKE PLAY: All the strokes for the round are counted.

SWEET SPOT: The area on the face of the club that strikes the ball perfectly.

TEEING GROUND: The starting area for the hole being played. Also referred to as the tee box. The teeing ground is a rectangular area, bordered in the front by two markers, and extending two club lengths in depth. The ball must be placed between the markers or back within two club lengths. The player may stand outside the teeing ground but the ball must be inside.

THROUGH THE GREEN: This is the whole area of the course except: (1) the teeing ground and putting green of the hole being played and (2) all hazards on the course.

UP: The number of holes a player is winning, 2 up and 3 holes to play.

USGA: United States Golf Association; the governing body of golf in America.

WATER HAZARD: Any sea, lake, pond, river, canal, ditch, or other open water within the confines of the course or adjacent to the course. Water hazards are marked by yellow stakes or yellow lines (see also "lateral water hazard").

WHIFF: A miss when attempting to hit the ball. This counts as a stroke.

WINTER RULES: Allows the golfer to improve the lie of the ball when the golf course is not in ideal shape.

Appendix B

Rules Simplified

These are just a few of the rules that will come up when you are golfing:
Every player tries to get around the 18 holes in as few a number of strokes as possible. The player must count every stroke whether they hit or miss the ball and that includes any "whiff" (see Golf Terms) or "fresh air" shot. If you swing with the intention of striking the ball, it is considered a stroke.

- Players may have to add a one-stroke or two-stroke penalty to the score. Become familiar with these penalties. All penalties must be added to the score as the infringement occurs.
- The player starts by teeing the ball between the markers on the teeing ground, which extends two club lengths back from the markers.
- When the player addresses the ball on the tee and the ball moves or falls off the tee there is no penalty. The ball is not yet in play and may be replaced without penalty.
- Elsewhere on the course if the ball moves after address, this is a one-stroke penalty and the ball must be replaced.
- If the player has not addressed the ball and it moves, no penalty occurs and the ball is played as it lies. If the player has not grounded the club, unless in a hazard, the player is not considered to have addressed the ball.
- If the player moves a loose impediment away from the ball through the green and the ball moves, a one-stroke penalty is incurred. The ball must be replaced. If the player removes something within one club length of the ball and the ball moves, a one-stroke penalty is also incurred. The ball must be replaced.
- If a player believes that a ball is lost or may be out of bounds, always play a provisional ball (see Golf Terms). If the original ball is found or is in bounds it must be played. The provisional will not count.
- When the ball is lost or goes out of bounds (see Golf Terms), the player must return to the spot where the previous ball was hit and drop another ball. You must count the stroke for the lost ball or out of bounds ball and add a penalty stroke.
- The ball may be dropped by standing erect and extending your arm horizontally at shoulder height and dropping it. The player may drop the ball to the side or directly out in front, provided it is not nearer the hole.
- If a ball goes into a hazard (see the rules in chapter 4), it may be played from the hazard; however, the player may not ground the club within the hazard. There is no penalty if you play the ball from the hazard but if you decide to drop out there is a one-stroke penalty.
- If the ball lands in the sand bunker, you may not place the sole of the club on the sand at address. The player must hold the club above the sand and then make the stroke. Infringement of this rule is a two-stroke penalty.

- The player may only remove anything that is human made from the bunker; for instance, a rake, a bottle, or a similar object. The player must not remove twigs or branches from the sand. Infringement of this rule is a two-stroke penalty.
- Through the green, if loose impediments are removed from beside the ball or within one club length of the ball and the ball moves, it is a one-stroke penalty. The ball must be replaced.
- On the green you should ask the opponent to put a coin or a marker behind their ball. If the opponent's ball is hit, it is a two-stroke penalty to you. You play your ball as it lies and replace the opponent's ball. The same penalty applies if you hit an attended or unattended flag while on the green. Remember if you remove the flag place it away from the line of the putt.
- If you chip or putt from off the green and hit the opponent's ball on the green, there is no penalty, and you play your ball as it lies. Replace the opponent's ball.
- Put a special identifying mark on your ball. Remember, if a player plays the wrong ball (except from a hazard) it is a two-stroke penalty.

It is imperative that everyone familiarize themselves with the rules of golf. There are a lot of rules, thus the necessity to carry an official rules book with you on the course. Some particular rules apply to match play and other rules to stroke play. An official rules book may be obtained from:

USGA
Golf House
P.O. Box 3000
Far Hills, NJ 07931–3000

SAMPLE RULES TEST

Helen and Liz are playing an 18-hole stroke play competition. Helen has 40 strokes and Liz has 37 strokes after the first nine. Please complete the final nine holes and determine the winner of the competition.
HANDICAP: Helen 8
          Liz 4

1. HOLE 10 Par 3
Helen has a par.
 A. 3
 B. 4
 C. 5
 D. 2

2. HOLE 10 Par 3
Liz has a birdie.
 A. 3
 B. 4
 C. 5
 D. 2

3. HOLE 11 Par 5

Helen's tee shot lands in a hazard bounded by yellow stakes or lines. She drops the ball in the usual manner. Her 3 wood lands in a bunker left of the green. She plays an explosion shot to within twenty feet of the flag. She 2 putts.

    A. 4
    B. 5
    C. 6
    D. 7

4. HOLE 11 Par 5

Liz stands outside the tee markers but places the ball between them. She hits her tee shot down the middle of the fairway. She addresses her ball in the fairway and it moves. She replaces it; from there she hits a 5 wood short of the green. She chips into the hole.

    A. 4
    B. 5
    C. 6
    D. 7
    E. 7

5. HOLE 12 Par 4

Helen hits her drive down the left side of the fairway. She hits a 5 wood onto the center of the green. She 2 putts.

    A. 5
    B. 4
    C. 6
    D. 7

6. HOLE 12 Par 4

Liz addresses the ball on the tee. The ball falls off the tee. She replaces it and hits a long drive down the middle of the fairway. Her 4 iron lands right of the green on the fringe. She putts and hits Helen's ball. She replaces Helen's ball and plays her own as it lies. She 2 putts.

    A. 5
    B. 6
    C. 8
    D. 7

7. HOLE 13 Par 5

Helen's tee shot lands very close to the out of bounds. She thinks that it may be out of bounds. She plays a provisional, which lands in the right rough. The ball was out of bounds. She hits the ball from the rough with the 7 wood; it lands 100 yards from the green. She uses a pitching wedge for her approach shot, which rolls to the back of the green and she 2 putts.

    A. 6
    B. 7
    C. 5
    D. 8

8. HOLE 13 Par 5

Liz hits her drive left; it lands at the base of a tree. She decides that it is unplayable and drops away from the tree in the correct manner. She hits a 3 wood short of the green. Her pitch shot lands ten feet from the hole. She drops the putt.

    A. 6
    B. 7
    C. 5
    D. 8

9. HOLE 14 Par 4

Helen hits her drive down the middle. Her second shot lands in the deep rough left of the green. She removes a branch from the ball. The ball moves, she replaces it. She plays a high pitch onto the green and 2 putts.

    A. 6
    B. 4
    C. 5
    D. 7

10. HOLE 14 Par 4

Liz uses her 3 wood from the tee. The ball lands in an ideal position to play her next shot. She takes out a 4 iron and plays a perfect shot to the center of the green. She 2 putts.

    A. 5
    B. 4
    C. 3
    D. 6

11. HOLE 15 Par 4

Helen hits the perfect drive. Her approach shot lands on the right half of the green. She putts and hits Liz's ball, which she replaces. She plays her own ball as it lies. She sinks the next putt.

    A. 5
    B. 4
    C. 6
    D. 7

12. HOLE 15 Par 4

Liz hits a poor drive, it lands near trees but is still in play. She takes a 7 iron to try to clear the trees; the ball hits a branch and may be lost. She plays a provisional, which lands 100 yards short of the green. The original 7 iron is lost. From 100 yards out she plays a great 9 iron to within 4 feet of the flag. She 1 putts.

    A. 4
    B. 5
    C. 7
    D. 6

13. HOLE 16 Par 4
Helen hits the green in regulation and 2 putts.
    A. 4
    B. 5
    C. 3
    D. 6

14. HOLE 16 Par 4
Liz hits the green in regulation. She repairs pitch marks on the line of her putt. She 3 putts.
    A. 4
    B. 5
    C. 3
    D. 6

15. HOLE 17 Par 3
Helen plays a 6 iron to the heart of the green and putts in regulation.
    A. 4
    B. 3
    C. 2
    D. 5

16. HOLE 17 Par 3
Liz hits a 6 iron that lands in ground under repair. She drops in the appropriate manner, not nearer the hole. She plays a pitching wedge, which flies over the green and lands on a grassy hill. She takes her stance, but does not ground the club. The ball moves, she plays it as it lies, and it lands thirty feet past the flag. She 2 putts.
    A. 3
    B. 6
    C. 5
    D. 7

17. HOLE 18 Par 4
Helen has a bogey.
    A. 5
    B. 4
    C. 6
    D. 7

18. HOLE 18 Par 4
Liz hits a long drive. Her next shot is pulled left of the green. She gets up and down from there.
    A. 5
    B. 4
    C. 6
    D. 7

19. A temporary accumulation of water is a
    A. water hazard.
    B. casual water.
    C. ground under repair.
    D. lateral water hazard.

20. If player presses down behind the ball to improve the lie, it is a penalty of
    A. one stroke.
    B. two stroke.
    C. There isn't a penalty.

21. A water hazard is marked by
    A. white markers.
    B. red markers.
    C. yellow markers.
    D. blue markers.

22. A lateral hazard is marked by
    A. red markers.
    B. yellow markers.
    C. white markers.
    D. blue markers.

23. Out of bounds is marked by
    A. white markers.
    B. red markers.
    C. yellow markers.
    D. blue markers.

24. Ground under repair is marked by
    A. white markers.
    B. red markers.
    C. yellow markers.
    D. blue markers.

25. While putting, if your ball strikes your opponents ball there is
    A. a one-stroke penalty.
    B. a two-stroke penalty.
    C. no penalty.
    D. disqualification.

26. If a player grounds a club in a hazard, there is
    A. no penalty.
    B. a one-stroke penalty.
    C. a two-stroke penalty.
    D. disqualification.

27. If a player removes a loose impediment within one club length of the ball and the ball moves, there is
    A. no penalty and the ball is replaced.
    B. a one-stroke penalty and the ball is replaced.
    C. no penalty and the ball is played as it lies.
    D. a one-stroke penalty and the ball is played as it lies.

28. If a player plays the wrong ball from the fairway and realizes the mistake four shots later while on the green, he or she is
    A. disqualified.
    B. given a one-stroke penalty.
    C. given no penalty but must go back and play from position of original ball.
    D. given a two-stroke penalty and must return to where his or her ball lies.

29. A player may drop a ball from shoulder height to the side or straight out in front provided the ball is not dropped nearer the hole.
    A. True
    B. False

30. Taking your stance and grounding the club is
    A. illegal.
    B. addressing the ball except in a hazard.
    C. hitting the ground with the club in a hazard.
    D. addressing the ball in a hazard.

Please answer questions 51 through 56 on the back of the scantron. One bonus point for each correct answer will be awarded for these questions.

51. Helen's gross score for 18 holes is
    A. 78.
    B. 79.
    C. 80.
    D. 84.
    E. None of the above.

52. Liz's gross score for 18 holes is
    A. 72.
    B. 77.
    C. 74.
    D. 75.
    E. Other.

53. Helen's net score is
    A. 69.
    B. 70.
    C. 76.
    D. 72.
    E. 73.

54. Liz has a net score of
    A. 69.
    B. 70.
    C. 71.
    D. 73.
    E. 74.

55. The winner of the medal competition is
    A. Helen.
    B. halved.
    C. Liz.

56. Fill in the scorecard and sign your name on it. Mark "A" on your scantron.

Answers: 1. A, 2. D, 3. C, 4. A, 5. B, 6. A, 7. B, 8. C, 9. A, 10. B, 11. C, 12. D, 13. A, 14. B, 15. B, 16. C, 17. A, 18. B, 19. B, 20. B, 21. C, 22. A, 23. A, 24. A, 25. B, 26. C, 27. B, 28. D, 29. A, 30. B

Answers on back of scantron: 51. D, 52. B, 53. C, 54. D, 55. C, 56. A

Appendix C

This wonderful practice for improving your overall game is thanks to its inventors Lynn Marriott and David Witt. The routine gives you the opportunity to practice with a purpose. You set a goal and when the task is completed you move to the next station. You may have reached your goal with a few balls or used all the balls trying to achieve the goal. When the bucket of balls has been used, you must move to the next station even if you have not reached the goal. If the requirements are too difficult for your ability, adjustments may be made or lower the standards set.

To lower your scores, practice the game the way it is scored. (63 percent short game, 37 percent full shots)

PUTTING

Make 3 6-foot putts, 2 putt from 30 feet 3 times, 2 putt from 60 feet 3 times.
Rules: One ball, one target. You move from the 6 foot putt to the 30 foot putt to the 60 foot putt; you make one attempt, whether successful or unsuccessful you move to next distance. If successful, you only need two more successes at that distance to achieve your goal. You must alternate; you may not remain at the same distance putt. The task is complete only when you have successfully holed out at each distance three times.

CHIPPING

Chip within 1-putt range 3 times to a short target.
Chip within 1-putt range 3 times to a long target.
Rules: Alternate short and long attempts until completed. This practice may take the whole bucket of thirty balls.
If unsuccessful and the bucket is empty, move on to the next task. You must alternate. If the goal is not reached, the task is completed when the thirty balls have been used.

PITCHING

Bucket: Thirty balls.
Same format as chipping; same rules apply.

SAND

Bucket: Thirty balls.
Same format as pitching and chipping; same rules apply.

FULL SHOTS

Bucket: Thirty balls.
Hit one perfect full sand wedge, hit one perfect full pitching wedge, hit one perfect 9 iron.
Choose two clubs out of the following: 8 iron through 3 wood; hit one perfect shot with each choice.
Hit two perfect tee shots.
Rules: You are allowed a maximum of thirty balls to complete all seven shots. You must savor and anchor each successful result. You must stop as you achieve each goal.

DAY 1

---

1. Keep a record of the length of time it takes to reach your goal on the putting green.
2. Keep records of the amount of balls needed to reach your goal chipping, pitching, and in sand play.
3. Keep a record of the number of balls needed to complete each task in the full swing. Was the entire bucket of thirty balls required to complete the task? Was the task incomplete and all the balls used?

DAY 2

Same as Day 1.

DAY 3

Same as Day 1.
Are you improving?

Suggested Readings

VIDEOTAPES

20 Problems 20 Solutions
60 min.
Jim McLean

Art of Putting
44 min.
Ben Crenshaw

Azinger on Fairway and Green Sand Traps
Couples on Tempo
20 min. each

David Leadbetter's Simple Secrets for Great Golf
70 min.

Full Swing
38 min.
Jack Nicklaus

Nick Faldo's Fixes
62 min.

Sixty Yards In
60 min.
Ray Floyd

The Short Game
65 min.
Seve Ballesteros

Women's Golf
A Window on the World
40 min.
Peggy Kirk Bell
De De Owens
Carolyn Hill
Annette Thompson
Muffin Spencer Devlin

Women's Golf
Mastering the Basics
40 min.
Annette Thompson
Michelle Bell

Sybervision: The Women's Game
60 min.
Patty Sheehan

Beginning Golf for Women
45 min.
Donna White

GENERAL INTEREST BOOKS

A Good Walk Spoiled
John Feinstein

Golf in the Kingdom
Michael Murphy

Little Red Book
Harvey Penick

And If You Play Golf, You Are My Friend
Harvey Penick

Norman: Advanced Golf
Greg Norman

Putt Like the Pros
Dave Pelz

Quantum Golf
Kjell Enhager

Watson's Rules of Golf
Tom Watson

Getting Up and Down
Tom Watson

Golf Is Not a Game of Perfect
Dr. Bob Rotella

Jack Grout's Golf Clinic
Annette Thompson
Introduction by Jack Nicklaus

BOOKS FOR WOMEN

For All Who Love the Game
Harvey Penick

Golf for Women: A Beginner's Guide
Dillon and Proctor

Golf for Women
Whitworth and Glenn

Play Golf the Wright Way
Mickey Wright

Amy Alcott's Guide to Women's Golf
Amy Alcott

Nancy Lopez's Complete Golfer
Nancy Lopez

Index

A

Addressing the ball, 52
Aerobic fitness, 146
Alignment/aim, 46, 51
Approach shot, 88

B

Backswing, 98–99
Ball flight, 117–124
    and beginning golfer, 123–124
    and club face position, 119–121
    and club path, 119, 120–121
    flight directions, 118
    problems/causes/corrections, 122–124
    and swing, 44–46
    and swing path, 118–119
Balls, choosing balls, 14
Bunker play, 22
    See also Sand shots
Bunkers (sand traps), 27, 28

C

Carts, 16
    safety, 40–41
Chipping, 22, 58, 75–85
    chipping to green, 77
    club choice, 76
    drills for, 80–83
    evaluation card for, 84
    and feel/confidence, 79
    performance checklist, 83
    principles of, 80
    stroke for, 76–79
Chip shot, 76
Clothing, 16–18
    footwear, 17
    gloves, 18
    waterproof suit, 18
Club face position, and ball flight,
    119–121
Club path, and ball flight, 119,
    120–121
Clubs. *See* Golf clubs

Commons, 3
Competition, types of, 36
Concentration, 151–152
Conditioning. *See* Mental conditioning;
    Physical conditioning
Confidence builder, 155
Crosswind, 140
Curving ball flights, 140–142
    draw, 141–142
    fade, 142

D

Disqualification, situations for, 35
Dogleg, 161–162
Downhill bunker shot, 130
Downhill lie, 137–138
Downswing, 43, 99–100, 102
Draw, 141–142
Driving range, 21–24
    safety on, 40

E

Etiquette, rules of, 37–39
Executive courses, 24
Explosion shot, 127–128

F

Fade, 141, 142
Fairway, 27, 28
Flag, 28, 163–164
Flexibility, 147–150
    exercises for, 147–150
Follow-through, 43, 100
"Fore," 40
Forecaddies, 3
Fourball, 36
Foursome, 36
Full swing, 96–116
    backswing/takeaway, 98–99
    downswing, 99–100, 102
    drills, 103–112
    follow-through, 100
    and hand position, 100–102

path/plane, importance of, 102
performance guidelines, 112
principles of, 104
and rhythm, 97
setup for, 97
and tempo, 97
top of backswing, 99

G

Game on course, 157–165
    guidelines for, 161–164
    and knowledge of skills, 158–160
Getting up and down from the green, 158
Gloves for golf, 18
Goal setting, 154–156
Golf
    history of, 2–3, 4
    information resources on, 183–185
    as lifetime sport, 4–5
    vacations, 5
Golf bags, 15
Golf clubs, 7–14
    club head lie, 9–10
    distance and hitting, 13–14
    grips, 8
    irons, 8, 11–12
    length of, 9
    parts of, 12
    putters, 12
    shaft flex, 8–9
    swing weight, 10
    woods, 8, 10
Golf course
    executive courses, 24
    first trip to, 24–25
    natural landscape of, 3
    safety on, 40–41
    trends related to, 3–4
    See also Game on course
Golf equipment
    balls, 14
    care of, 18–19
    carts, 16
    clubs, 7–14
    golf bags, 15
    tees, 15

Gorse, 3
Green, 27, 28
Grip, 46, 47, 48–50
    guidelines for, 48–50
    and putting, 58–59
    types of grips, 49–50
Grips of golf clubs, 8
Grounding the club, sand shots, 126

H

Handicaps, 35–36
Hazards, 27
    sand bunker, 126
    water hazards, 27, 28, 32–33
Head wind, 138–139
Heather, 3
Heaths, 3
Hilly lies. *See* Uneven lies
Hole, 27, 28
    par of, 29
Honor, 37
Hook, 44, 45

I

Inswing principles, 46–47
Interlock grip, 49
Irons, 8, 11–12

L

Lateral water hazard, 27, 32–33
Learning game
    driving ranges, 21–24
    first trip to course, 24–25
    from professionals, 21
Links, 3
Long pitch, 90–91
Lost ball, 31
LPGA (Ladies Professional Golf
    Association), 21

M

Match play, 36
Medal play, 36

Mental conditioning
    attitude, 152
    concentration, 151–152
    relaxation methods, 150–151
    self-confidence, 151

O

One-stroke penalty, 30–34
Out of bounds, 28, 29, 31
Overlap grip, 50

P

Par, of hole, 29
Par golf, 22
Parkland, 3
Penalties, 29–35
    disqualification, 35
    no penalty, 30
    one-stroke penalty, 30–34
    two-stroke penalty, 34–35
PGA (Professional Golf Association), 21
Physical conditioning
    aerobic fitness, 146
    flexibility, 147–150
    strength training, 146–147
Pitching, 59, 87–95
    approach shot, 88
    drills, 92–94
    from long grass, 92
    long pitch, 90–91
    performance checklist, 95
    pitch shot, 88
    principles of, 92
    short pitch, 88–90
Plug mark, repair of, 38
Preswing principles
    for putting, 61–62
    for swing, 46, 52–53
Punch shot, 138, 139
Putters, 12
    areas of course for use, 29
Putting, 22, 57–73
    for distance, 63
    drills for, 64–70
    and grip, 58–59

    preswing routine, 61–62
    principles of, 61
    and reading the green, 62–63
    setup for, 59–60, 64
    simplicity in, 58–59
    stroke, 60–61
    uphill/downhill/sidehill
        putts, 63
Putting green, 28

R

Reading the green, 62–63, 164
Regular water hazard, 27
Regulation, 158
    for putting, 58, 59
Relaxation methods, 150–151
Reverse overlap grip, 58–59
Rhythm, and full swing, 97
Rough, 27, 28
Rules of golf
    etiquette, 37–39
    penalties, 29–35
    rules, 29

S

Safety, 39–41
    on course, 40–41
    on driving range, 40
    and weather, 40
Sand shots, 125–133
    buried lie, 128
    and confidence, 126
    downhill bunker shot, 130
    drills, 131–132
    explosion shot, 127–128
    fairway bunker shot, 130
    grounding the club, 126
    performance guidelines, 130
    principles of sand play, 129
    uphill bunker shot, 128, 130
Sand traps, 27, 28
Sand wedge, 127
Scorecard, 37
Setup, 46, 50–51
    ball placement for, 50–51

Shaft flex, golf clubs, 8–9
Shoes for golf, 17
Short pitch, 88–90
Sidehill lie, 135–137
Singles, 36
Slice, 44, 45
Strength training, 146–147
Stroke, putting, 60–61
Stroke play, 36
Swing, 42–56
    addressing the ball, 52
    and alignment, 51
    and ball flight laws, 44–46
    factors affecting swing, 43–44
    full swing, 96–116
    and grip, 48–50
    inswing principles, 46–47
    practice guidelines, 52–53
    preswing principles, 46, 52–53
    and setup, 50–51
Swing center, 47
Swing weight, golf clubs, 10

T

Tail wind, 139
Takeaway, 43, 98–99
Target line, 98, 99
Tee, 15, 27
Teeing area, 27, 28
Tempo, and full swing, 97
Ten-finger grip, 49

Threesome, 36
Two-stroke penalty, 34–35

U

Uneven lies, 134–144
    curving ball flights, 140–142
    downhill lie, 137–138
    drills for, 142–144
    performance checklist, 138
    punch shot, 138
    sidehill lie, 135–137
    uphill lie, 137
    and wind, 138–140
United States Golf Association (USGA)
    slope and index rating system,
    35–36
Unplayable lie, 31
Uphill bunker shot, 128, 130
Uphill lie, 137

W

Water hazards, 27, 28, 32
    lateral water hazard, 27, 32–33
Waterproof suit, 18
Weather, 40
Wind, 138–140
    crosswind, 140
    head wind, 138–139
    tail wind, 139
Woods, 8, 10
    areas of course for use, 29